FEED YOUR FAMILY FOR UNDER A FIV£R

OVER 80 EASY, BUDGET-FRIENDLY RECIPES

MITCH LANE

Thorsons

WHEN USING KITCHEN APPLIANCES PLEASE ALWAYS
FOLLOW THE MANUFACTURER'S INSTRUCTIONS

HarperCollins*Publishers*
1 London Bridge Street
London SE1 9GF
www.harpercollins.co.uk

HarperCollins*Publishers*
Macken House, 39/40 Mayor Street Upper
Dublin 1, D01 C9W8, Ireland

First published by HarperCollins*Publishers* 2023

1 3 5 7 9 10 8 6 4 2

Text © Mitch Lane 2023
Photography © Tom Regester 2023

Mitch Lane asserts the moral right to be identified
as the author of this work

A catalogue record of this book is available
from the British Library

ISBN 978-0-00-860043-3

Photographer: Tom Regester
Food Stylist: Esther Clark
Prop Stylist: Max Robinson

Printed and bound at GPS Group, Slovenia

MIX
Paper | Supporting
responsible forestry
FSC™ C007454

FSC
www.fsc.org

This book is produced from independently certified FSC™
paper to ensure responsible forest management.

For more information visit: www.harpercollins.co.uk/green

FEED YOUR FAMILY FOR UNDER A FIV£R

```
GARLIC BULB SINGLE        £0.20
JS FRESH BASIL            £0.60
JS RED CHILLIES 60G       £0.70
JS CHERRY TOMS 330G       £0.90
JS PRMIGIANO RG SHKR      £1.45
JS PENNE                  £0.95

6 BALANCE DUE             £4.80
  Mastercard              4.80
  contactless ))) 
```

PLEASE KEEP FOR YOUR RECORDS
PUBLISHED TERMS AND CONDITIONS APPLY

Thank you for your visit.

```
HUBBARDS PLUM TOMS        £0.28
JS FUSILLI 500G           £0.85
JS 38 CHORIZO SLICES      £1.34
JS PARSLEY 30G            £0.60
JS RED CHILLIES 60G       £0.70
ONIONS RED LSE
0.140 kg @    £0.75/kg    £0.11
M ANN DMZARELLA 125G      £0.45
M ANN DMZARELLA 125G      £0.45
GARLIC BULB SINGLE        £0.20

9 BALANCE DUE             £4.98
  CASH                    £5.00

  CHANGE                  £0.02
***********************************
```

Thank you for your visit.

```
BABYLEAF SPINACH 100      £1.30
ONIONS LOOSE
0.144 kg @    £0.65/kg    £0.09
JS CORIANDER 30G          £0.50
HUBBARDS CHOPD TOMS       £0.28
GINGER LOOSE
0.012 kg @    £5.25/kg    £0.06
BAKING POTATOES LOOS
0.215 kg @    £0.60/kg    £0.13
JS HOT CURRY POWDER       £1.30
ONIONS LOOSE
0.126 kg @    £0.65/kg    £0.08
BAKING POTATOES LOOS
0.220 kg @    £0.60/kg    £0.13
CARROTS LOOSE
0.118 kg @    £0.45/kg    £0.05
CARROTS LOOSE
0.098 kg @    £0.45/kg    £0.04
GARLIC BULB SINGLE        £0.20
JS RED CHILLIES 60G       £0.70
GREENGROCER PEAS          £0.52

14 BALANCE DUE            £4.88
  CLSVISA                 £4.88
  contactless )))
```

```
GBP
49486 Honey 340g          0.75 A
700161 Cinnamon GROUND    0.59 A
82111 Blueberries 400G    1.89 A
85099 Oats Porridge 1kg   0.70 A
63893 *Whole Milk         0.85 A


Total            4.78
5 Items
Card Sales        GBP4.78
```

```
JS PLAIN FLOUR            £0.55
JS DOUBLE CRM 150ML       £0.50
JS BAKING POWDER          £1.00
JS GRANU SUGAR            £0.55
JS BELGIAN CHOC           £1.10
JS GROUND CINNAMON        £0.85

6 BALANCE DUE             £4.55
  CASH                   £10.00

  CHANGE                  £5.45
***********************************
```

```
C       #5155    12:01:24  02JUL2022
```

```
GARLIC BULB SINGLE        £0.25
IMP TASTY LEMONS X5       £0.63
JS MIXED HERBS            £0.85
CHICKEN WINGS             £1.75
JS PARSLEY 30G            £0.60

5 BALANCE DUE             £4.08
  CLSVISA                 £4.08
```

PLEASE KEEP FOR YOUR RECORDS
PUBLISHED TERMS AND CONDITIONS APPLY

```
JS CHICKEN LEG 1KG        £1.99
CARROTS LOOSE
0.212 kg @    £0.47/kg    £0.10
ONIONS SPRING BUNCH       £0.49
GARLIC BULB SINGLE        £0.20
JS DOUBLE CRM 150ML       £0.90
JS SOL PUFF PASTRY        £1.25

6 BALANCE DUE             £4.93
  CLSVISA                 £4.93
  contactless )))
```

PLEASE KEEP FOR YOUR RECORDS
PUBLISHED TERMS AND CONDITIONS APPLY

```
JS BEEF STOCK CUBES
JS 20% FAT MINCE
PEPPER YELLOW
GARLIC BULB SINGLE        £0.20
HUBBARDS PLUM TOMS        £0.28
JS HOT CHILLI MIX         £0.55
HUBBARDS TMATO SAUCE      £0.25
ONIONS LOOSE
0.208 kg @    £0.65/kg    £0.14
JS RD/KIDNY BEAN          £0.50

9 BALANCE DUE             £4.96
  Mastercard              £4.96
```

Thank you for your visit.

```
ISB CHEESE BATON          £0.70
COCONUT MILK LIGHT        £1.00
ONIONS RED LSE
0.222 kg @    £0.75/kg    £0.17
JS MEDIUM CURRY           £1.10
JS RED CHILLIES 60G       £0.70
GINGER LOOSE
0.018 kg @    £5.25/kg    £0.09
JS VEGETABLE STOCK C      £0.65
IMTASTY CARROTS 1KG       £0.35
GARLIC BULB SINGLE        £0.20

9 BALANCE DUE             £4.96
  Mastercard              £4.96
  contactless )))
```

PLEASE KEEP FOR YOUR RECORDS
PUBLISHED TERMS AND CONDITIONS APPLY

Contents

Introduction

I'm Mitch.

I'm from Wolverhampton, a father of three kids and head chef of my home kitchen. I am the Mitch in @mealsbymitch from TikTok and Instagram and I'm here to show you how to cook some incredible homemade food on a budget.

. . . .

Times are tough at the moment. The cost of living is rising higher and higher, the price of food is constantly going up, and we are all one step closer to the breadline month by month. That's where this book comes in; I want you all to be able to enjoy tasty, comforting and indulgent food without having to dig too deeply into your pockets. So often I see recipes with ingredients that you'd practically need to take out a mortgage or bank loan to buy, and for most of us these are just not practical in the current climate.

. . . .

So I've stripped these recipes back to the bare bones and taken some cheap and humble ingredients and turned them into something special. Some foods might be cheap to buy, but that doesn't mean they need to taste cheap!

I've lived on a budget for most of my life and I've fed my family on all these meals at some point. You only need a fiver to make each recipe – although with prices constantly increasing, it's hard to know how long they will stay within that budget. Hopefully they will stand the test of time!

Every recipe in this book is centred around you being able to walk into a shop or supermarket with a fiver in your pocket and come out with everything you need to make the meal of your choice for a family of four. All I'm expecting you to have in your cupboards is some salt and pepper and some cooking oil (vegetable oil, olive oil, and so on) – everything else is included in the budget! There are recipes for everything, including budget pasta dishes, cheap breakfasts, homemade soups, British classics, curries, one-pot wonders and sweet stuff – you only live once after all.

No equipment necessary.
No space? No problem

The reality is that my kitchen at home is *tiny* – I can touch the walls on both sides with outspread arms. I've seen pantries or utility rooms bigger than my kitchen. But the beauty of these recipes is that you don't need a big and extravagant kitchen with state-of-the-art equipment to be able to cook up a storm. In defence of all small kitchens out there it's nice to have everything close by and at your fingertips without having to run a half marathon to get to each cupboard and appliance. So what I'm trying to say is that I've based these recipes on using basic kitchen essentials. You don't need anything fancy.

A few of the recipes need a deep-fat fryer, but if you don't have one you can use an ordinary saucepan to heat the oil and a basic cooking thermometer to tell you how hot it is. Follow the instructions in the recipes and you should be fine. When you've finished deep frying, allow the oil to cool completely, then store it in a plastic container in a cool, dry place to use again. You can reuse cooking oil like this five or six times, but discard it (take it to a recycling centre, don't pour it down the sink or it will block your drain) when it becomes dark in colour.

Anyone with any cooking ability will be able to attempt these recipes. It doesn't matter if you're a complete novice; they are all simple and easy to follow. You don't need any finesse or culinary experience; all you need is an able pair of hands and a willingness to try new things. Absolutely anybody can cook – think about it in simple terms; all we are doing is putting some ingredients into a pan or baking tray at the right times. We're not overcomplicating it, so don't be afraid to give it a go!

How to make your fiver go further – essential shopping tips

Now look, we're cooking on a budget. The harsh reality is that we're not going to be able to afford extravagant cuts of meat, branded items or organic veggies and fruit, and so on. They would take us well over budget unfortunately! So here are a few tips to keep your meals within budget:

- We need to get into a meal-for-a-fiver meal mindset and make that budget stretch. You need to buy 'wonky' or 'imperfect' ranges of fruit and veggies when possible. Carrots don't have to look like a typical carrot to taste like a carrot. Also, try to buy vegetables separately, as a single onion or bulb of garlic often works out cheaper than buying them prepacked. If you have a local market with a fruit and vegetable stall, check out their prices too – stallholders can often undercut supermarkets in price as they buy what's available on the day. They also offer large, low-priced bowls of fruit or vegetables (such as mushrooms) that need to be eaten in the next day or so.

- Never go into a supermarket on an empty stomach. If you're walking down the aisles feeling hungry, you'll end up buying a lot of junk food that you wouldn't normally put in the trolley! So make sure you've eaten before you go shopping.

- I recommend making a plan of action and a list before going shopping; plan your meals for the week and know exactly what you're going to be eating before you set foot through the door.

- In a supermarket buy own brand items, such as tinned food (tomatoes, beans, sweetcorn and so on.)

Although I've based each meal on a fiver, that doesn't mean five meals will cost you £25 – the total is likely to be much less because a lot of ingredients can be used in several different recipes! You will find some recipes have an 'In The Basket' box. This is just to provide more information on how much of an ingredient I was able to buy for the £5 budget.

For example, if a recipe requires beef stock, I've based the costs on buying a whole packet of stock cubes, so you'll end up saving money on the next recipe that needs stock! The same applies to seasonings, bags of flour, and so on.

All I say is that if you don't have a lot of money don't think for a second that you have to live on rubbish microwave meals or instant noodles. Push the boat out a bit and have a go at cooking one of these meals from scratch; treat your family to something different. Don't be concerned about trying new things or stepping out of your comfort zone.

I've put my heart and soul into this book, and I hope you'll find something you love in it.

Mitch

Breakfast

Chorizo Hash

What a way to start your day! This one is just so good – it has so many different flavours and textures going on that it will definitely become one of your top three breakfasts *ever*! Heat from the chilli, crunch from the pepper and spring onions, comforting bites of heaven from the potatoes – and don't get me started on those sunny-side-up runny egg yolks to dip everything into! It's a properly naughty breakfast that I keep making. I'm drooling just thinking about it.

Ingredients

1 tbsp vegetable or olive oil
180g thin chorizo slices, roughly chopped
4 baking potatoes, cut into 2cm chunks
1 onion, diced
1 red pepper, diced
½ red chilli, finely chopped (deseeded for a milder dish),
6 eggs (1–2 per serving)
4 spring onions, finely chopped, to serve
salt and pepper

Method

1. Start by putting a frying pan on a medium heat, then add the oil along with the chorizo pieces. Let them cook for 2 minutes until they start to release their oils and juices. Take them out of the pan and set aside.

2. Add the potato chunks to the pan and let them cook and soften in the chorizo juices. Try to ensure that every piece of potato makes contact with the pan because you want them all nicely coloured. Turn them over periodically. Be patient with this stage; it will take at least 10 minutes for the potatoes to begin to soften.

3. Add the onion and pepper along with the chilli and continue to cook for 5 minutes. Keep stirring once every minute.

4. After 5 minutes the potatoes should be beautifully soft, but also golden and crisp on the outside. At this stage add salt and pepper, return the chorizo and mix well. Take everything out of the pan and set aside.

5. Crack the eggs (as many or as few as you like) into the same pan and cook them to your liking. Of course for this dish you want a properly indulgent runny yolk!

6. Top the eggs in the pan with the chorizo hash to warm through. Sprinkle with spring onions, grind a few cracks of black pepper over the top and serve.

Cinnamon and Blueberry Porridge

Porridge is the king of budget breakfasts and the beauty of it is that it's just so versatile. You can buy a 1kg bag for less than 80p (at the time of writing) – enough oats to make this recipe five times! I've based this one on blueberries but you could easily swap them for mixed berries or strawberries. You could even add a drop of vanilla to the oats as they are warming up for another flavour. The blueberry and cinnamon combo works a treat though so it is definitely my go to.

VEGETARIAN

Ingredients

400g frozen blueberries
200g porridge oats
568ml milk
1 tsp cinnamon, plus extra to serve
10 tbsp honey, plus extra for
    drizzling

Method

1. Put a pan on a low heat and add the frozen blueberries. Let them soften for 8–10 minutes.
2. While the blueberries are softening, put a separate pan on a medium heat and add the oats, milk, cinnamon, honey and 300ml water. Bring the mixture to a simmer and then keep stirring it for 4–5 minutes until it thickens and softens.
3. Serve the oats in four bowls, spoon over the softened blueberries and drizzle over the blueberry juice from the bottom of the pan. I like to make some pretty patterns.
4. Drizzle over another teaspoon of honey and a small dusting of cinnamon and serve.

IN THE BASKET

OATS: based on 1kg bag

CINNAMON: based on full jar

HONEY: based on 340g jar

Loaded Scrambled Eggs

Would you believe that scrambled eggs can be quite versatile? You can load them up with pretty much anything you like. These are quite simple, but they're everything you want when it comes to a breakfast meal! This properly sets you up for the day – trust me on that; with melted cheese, a few pops of crunch from the pepper, onion and a nice little kick from the chilli! Deseed the chilli for a milder dish.

VEGETARIAN

Ingredients

2 tbsp vegetable or olive oil
1 red onion, diced
½ green chilli, finely chopped, plus slices to serve
1 red pepper, diced
12 medium eggs
100g Cheddar cheese, grated
salt and pepper

Method

1. Put a frying pan on a medium heat and add half the oil, along with the onion, chilli and red pepper. Cook for 3–4 minutes until they begin to soften. When cooked, set them aside for later.

2. Turn down the heat to low and add the remaining oil before cracking in the eggs. (I like to use butter rather than oil for the best results, but the cost of living crisis doesn't allow for butter!)

3. Keep moving the eggs around the pan. I use a rubber spatula to avoid scratching the pan. Keep scraping the bottom and sides of the pan to ensure that no egg is sticking. Everybody in my house likes their scrambled eggs cooked differently, so only you will know when the eggs are cooked to your liking. The whole cooking process should take 3–4 minutes.

4. Add the cheese to the pan and return the onion, pepper and chilli. Give everything a good mix for 10–15 seconds until the cheese has melted. Season with salt and pepper to taste.

5. Serve with sliced green chilli.

IN THE BASKET

CHEESE: based on 220g block

Spicy Avocado Toast

This is a super-quick breakfast that you can chuck together in ten minutes. It's completely effortless and quite an indulgent plate of food too. So if you want to impress your partner with an elegant bit of breakfast in bed, then you're in the right place! Avocados never really scream budget, but you will be surprised at what you can get for your money if you keep your eyes peeled in the supermarket. I'm turning these avocados into something similar to a guacamole and paired with some toasted, thick-cut slices of seeded bloomer loaf it tastes incredible. You can tweak the heat level to your taste by adjusting the amount of chilli. I base this on half a chilli but if you're a spice lover, then add a whole one – or even two. If you prefer a milder dish, deseed the chilli.

VEGETARIAN

Ingredients

1 seeded white bloomer loaf, cut into 2cm thick slices

3 medium avocados, peeled and stoned

½ green chilli, finely chopped, plus slices to serve

1 tomato, finely chopped

½ red onion, finely chopped, plus slices to serve

10g fresh coriander, chopped, plus extra to serve

juice of 1 lime

salt and pepper

Method

1. Toast the slices of bread. I toast mine in a griddle pan which gives them some nice black char marks.

2. In a bowl combine the avocado flesh, chilli, tomato, red onion and coriander. Add the lime juice and then mash everything up with the back of a fork until it is quite smooth.

3. Add salt and pepper and then taste it. Adjust the seasoning and spice level to suit you.

4. Spread the guacamole on the toast and serve with sliced chillies, thinly-sliced red onion rings and a few coriander leaves.

Cheesy Spinach Stuffed Mushrooms on Toast

This is not a traditional breakfast meal but it's the way I want to start my day pretty much every single day. Creamy, cheesy and garlicky! You don't need any skill to put this one together; it's very simple and you can cook it in half an hour (including prep). I've even included some bread in the budget so you can toast it for a different texture, or cut it into small pieces and dip it into the cheese and spinach mixture!

VEGETARIAN

Ingredients

8 large flat mushrooms, stalks removed
1 tbsp olive oil
2 garlic cloves, finely chopped
100g fresh spinach leaves
200g cream cheese
125g mozzarella ball
1 white bread baton
salt and pepper

Method

1. Preheat the oven to 180°C/160°C fan/gas mark 4. Place the mushrooms on a baking tray with the stalk side facing upwards, and set aside for later.

2. Put a frying pan on a low heat and add the oil and garlic. Keep moving the garlic around the pan, ensuring it doesn't burn; you don't want it to colour. Cook it for 1 minute.

3. Add the spinach leaves and cook for a further 2 minutes until it has wilted.

4. Put the spinach and garlic into a bowl along with the cream cheese and some salt and pepper. Mix them together until well combined.

5. Spoon the mixture into the mushroom tops. Break the ball of mozzarella into small pieces and place them on top of the mushrooms. Bake the mushrooms in the oven for 20 minutes.

6. While the mushrooms are cooking, toast the baton. Cut it in half lengthways and toast in a griddle pan or toaster.

7. Serve the mushrooms piping hot on the toasted bread. They will release a lot of their water on to the baking tray so take care when removing it from the oven.

Salmon and Cucumber Bagels

Believe it or not you can afford to make some pretty posh salmon bagels on a budget – I didn't believe it at first but you can keep this cheap by buying salmon trimmings. Are they any less tasty than a prime cut of salmon? Not really. Is it going to be kind to your bank balance though? Absolutely. The only cooking in this recipe is toasting the bagels and then putting the indulgent toppings on top. It really is a five-minute job so if you're up late but still want a good bit of breakfast in you, this is the right recipe for you.

Ingredients

4 bagels, sliced in half
200g cream cheese
juice of ½ lemon
½ cucumber
100g smoked salmon trimmings
salt and pepper

Method

1. Start by toasting the bagel halves in a griddle pan or toaster.
2. Put the cream cheese, lemon juice and some salt and pepper into a bowl. Give them all a good mix.
3. Grab a potato peeler and peel long shavings of cucumber. You want them to be thin, delicate and elegant – although this is a cheap dish, we want it to be pleasing to the eye!
4. Once the bagels are toasted; spread them with some of the cream cheese mixture, layer on the cucumber shavings and then top with a generous quantity of smoked salmon. It's incredibly simple, but looks and tastes fantastic.

Corned Beef Hash

If you only have a fiver to your name then you're on to a winner with this one. Top this dish with a couple of fried eggs and you've got some serious comfort food! I'm a firm believer that corned beef is a million times better when you cook it. I've never been a fan of it cold in a sandwich, but the second you warm it up in a dish like this, then all of a sudden it becomes a top-tier tasting meat. It doesn't seem to get the love it deserves. Incredibly cheap, but properly comforting.

Ingredients

2 tbsp vegetable or olive oil

4 large baking potatoes, skin on, chopped into 2cm chunks

1 onion, finely chopped

1 x 340g tin corned beef, cut into 2cm chunks

1 tsp paprika

1 tbsp Worcestershire sauce

4 eggs

a few chives, finely chopped, to serve (optional)

salt and pepper

Method

1. Put a frying pan on a medium heat and add half of the oil. Add the potatoes and ensure that they all make contact with the pan. Try to avoid moving them around to begin with; you want them to turn a nice golden colour. Leave them to cook for 5 minutes.

2. Add the onion and continue to cook for 3 minutes. Add the corned beef, together with the paprika and some salt and pepper, and let everything cook for another 2 minutes. Add the Worcestershire sauce and give it one final stir. By this point the potatoes should be nice and tender.

3. Take the corned beef hash out of the pan and plate it up. Pour the second tablespoon of oil into the same pan and crack in the eggs. Keep your eye on them: you're aiming for beautifully sunny-side-up eggs with runny yolks.

4. When the eggs are cooked, lay them on top of the corned beef hash and sprinkle with the chives, if using.

IN THE BASKET

PAPRIKA: based on full jar

WORCESTERSHIRE SAUCE: based on full bottle

EGGS: based on box of 6

Breakfast Quesadillas

Recipes really don't get much simpler than this; trust me – four-ingredient breakfast quesadillas that are a treat first thing in the morning. It's a Saturday morning ritual in my house to make these and every time I do my kids devour the entire plate. This is the *only* way to start a Saturday and sets you up perfectly for the day.

Ingredients

8 slices of bacon (1 x 250g pack)
6 eggs
1 tbsp vegetable or olive oil
4 plain wraps
150g Red Leicester or Cheddar
    cheese, grated
ketchup or sauce, optional

Method

1. Preheat the oven to 180°C/160°C fan/gas mark 4.
2. Layer the bacon slices on a baking tray and put it into the oven for 15 minutes or until the bacon is cooked to your liking. I prefer my bacon crispy. Once the bacon is cooked, roughly chop it into little pieces and set aside.
3. Crack the eggs into a bowl, and whisk with a fork until they are smooth and the yolks and whites are completely mixed.
4. Put a frying pan on a medium heat, add the oil and then a quarter of the beaten egg mixture. Gently move the eggs around the pan, ensuring that they coat the entire surface of the pan.
5. After 20–30 seconds the eggs will begin to set; at this point add a wrap to the pan, cook for 30 seconds and then flip the wrap and eggs over. You'll notice that the eggs will stick to the wrap.
6. Put 50g of the cheese on the right-hand side of the wrap, along with a third of the chopped bacon. You can also add some ketchup or sauce of your choice at this stage.
7. Very carefully fold over the wrap so the cheese and bacon are sandwiched in the middle (it will resemble a traditional quesadilla at this stage).
8. Leave the quesadilla in the pan for a further 30–45 seconds to allow the cheese to melt and the wrap to crisp on the outside and take on some colour.
9. Take the wrap out of the pan, cut it into three triangles and it is ready to serve. Repeat the process three more times to make four quesadillas.

IN THE BASKET

WRAPS: based on pack of 8

CHEESE: based on 400g pack

Shakshuka

If you fancy something a little different for breakfast and are sick of the usual cereals and toast, then I recommend giving this one a go! The flavours in this will slap you in the face and soon wake you up. You won't even need that morning cup of coffee – trust me on this! And the best part about it is that it's all cooked in one pan so there's hardly any messing about at all.

VEGETARIAN

Ingredients

1 tsp vegetable or olive oil

1 onion, diced

1 red pepper, diced

5 garlic cloves, finely chopped

1 tsp paprika

½ tsp ground cumin

400g tin chopped tomatoes

6 eggs

fresh coriander or parsley,
   chopped, to serve

1 crusty roll

salt and pepper

Method

1. Put a frying pan with a lid on a medium high heat and add the oil, then the onion and red pepper and let them soften for 4–5 minutes.

2. Add the garlic, paprika and cumin and cook for a further 2 minutes, then add the tomatoes and give everything a stir.

3. Make five wells in the tomato mixture, each big enough to hold an egg. Crack an egg into each well, then put on the pan lid and cook for about 3 minutes. Keep checking on the eggs every minute as they cook extremely fast with the lid on (the tops steam inside the pan and the last thing you want for this dish is a hard yolk)!

4. When the eggs are cooked but still have a beautifully runny yolk, add salt and pepper and sprinkle with your chosen herb.

5. Chop up the crusty roll for dipping, and you're ready to serve! I serve this straight from the pan for a rustic feel and most of the time I can't be bothered with the washing up so that saves on plates as well!

IN THE BASKET

PAPRIKA: based on full jar

CUMIN: based on full jar

Chocolate French Toast with Caramelised Bananas

Some of you may know this as eggy bread, although this is a sweeter version! I can't make my mind up whether this is a breakfast or a dessert. It really doesn't matter either way because I could happily sit and eat this at 3 o'clock in the morning. As far as bang for your buck goes, this is a winner; there will be loads of ingredients left over so you can just keep making more and more! Traditionally, we should use brioche rather than white bread, but if we're on a budget we're going to have to settle for thick-cut white bread! Does that make it any less indulgent? Absolutely not.

VEGETARIAN

Ingredients

6 medium eggs
2 heaped tbsp brown sugar
2 tsp ground cinnamon
10 tbsp milk
8 slices white bread
4 tbsp vegetable oil
100g milk chocolate, broken into pieces
2 bananas, peeled and sliced lengthways
1 tbsp brown sugar
2 tbsp icing sugar, for dusting

Method

1. Put the eggs, brown sugar, cinnamon and milk into a bowl. Whisk everything together until nicely combined.

2. One by one dip the bread slices in the bowl, fully submerging each one it so it soaks up the milk and eggs. You want each slice to be completely covered.

3. Put a frying pan on a medium heat and add 2 tablespoons of the oil. Carefully add 2 slices of the soaked bread and cook them for about 2 minutes until golden and crisp. Keep your eye on the pan as they can burn very quickly! After 2 minutes, flip over the bread and add 25g (a quarter) of the chocolate to one slice. Let it cook on the second side for 2 minutes, then lay the slices on top of each other to make a chocolate sandwich.

4. Repeat this process to make the remaining 3 portions.

5. Put the brown sugar on a plate and coat the banana pieces in sugar on both sides.

6. Use the a toast pan to fry the bananas and allow them to caramelise for 2 minutes on each side.

7. Now it's time to serve; put the French toast on the plate first, followed by a dusting of icing sugar and then place the caramelised bananas on top.

🧺 IN THE BASKET

SUGAR: based on 1kg bag
CINNAMON: based on full jar
MILK: based on 1 pint bottle
BREAD: based on 800g loaf
ICING SUGAR: based on 500g bag

Blueberry Pancakes

I'm classing this as a breakfast, because what better way is there to start your day than with some of the fluffiest pancakes you've ever eaten? Every now and again as you eat them you will pop a juicy blueberry and that is so heavenly. I suppose you could eat these any time of day. If you need an excuse, it's always breakfast time somewhere in the world! If you want to swap the blueberries for a different fruit then you can – bananas work really well too! What I love about this recipe is that if you buy all the ingredients below, there will be plenty left over to make it a second time (all you'd have to do is buy more blueberries). Start by measuring out your ingredients as accurately as possible so you have everything at your fingertips before you start.

VEGETARIAN

Ingredients

250g plain flour
70g granulated sugar
2 tsp baking powder
½ tsp salt
230ml milk
3 medium eggs
a few drops vanilla essence (optional)
125g blueberries (from a budget range)
1 tbsp vegetable oil

IN THE BASKET

FLOUR: based on 1.5kg bag

SUGAR: based on 1kg bag

BAKING POWDER: based on full tub

MILK: based on 1 pint bottle

EGGS: based on box of 6

Method

1. Grab a mixing bowl and put in the flour, sugar, baking powder and salt. Give them all a good mix until combined.
2. Pour the milk into a jug and crack in the eggs. Whisk until they are combined.
3. Gradually pour the milk and egg mixture into the dry mixture, mixing all the time. It's easier to use an electric whisk for this part. If you don't own one use a handheld one and be prepared for a work out! Add the vanilla essence, if using.
4. When you have a nice batter consistency, add the blueberries and give the mixture one final stir. Now it's time to cook the pancakes; traditionally we'd use butter for this but as butter costs a small fortune these days a neutral oil is a good substitute. Put a frying pan on a medium heat, add the oil, and ladle in the batter mixture (1 ladle for a small pancake or 2 ladles for a big one). Keep your eye on them; they will go from golden brown to burned in the blink of an eye. They should cook in about 2 minutes on each side. You're looking for a golden brown crust with a fluffy inside.
5. Repeat until you have used up all the batter and serve the pancakes hot. Use extra blueberries to serve if liked.

soups

Chunky Mexican Mixed Bean Soup

What an absolute beaut of a winter warmer this one is – a nice little kick of spice that instantly warms you on a cold day. I didn't know meat-free dishes could taste this good, but they do and I'll go as far as saying that this is one of my top three favourite soups. This recipe is a great example of how to turn very average tins of beans and sweetcorn into a showstopper soup! I use a ready-made fajita spice mix, but if you have cumin, chilli powder, paprika, dried garlic, oregano and parsley in your cupboard, then use them instead. Best part? You only need one pan. Absolute winner.

VEGETARIAN

Ingredients

1 tbsp vegetable or olive oil
1 onion, roughly chopped
1 yellow or orange pepper, roughly chopped
4 garlic cloves, finely chopped
28g Mexican fajita seasoning
400g tin chopped tomatoes
157g tin sweetcorn, drained
130g tin kidney beans, drained
130g tin butter beans, drained
1 litre vegetable stock (made from a stock cube)
15g fresh coriander, finely chopped, plus extra for serving
juice of ½ lime
salt and pepper

Method

1. Put a large pan on a medium heat and add the oil followed by the onion and pepper and a pinch of salt. Let them soften for 2–3 minutes. Add the garlic, continue to cook for 1 minute, then add the seasoning and stir it through for 30 seconds.

2. Add the tinned stuff: tip in the tomatoes, sweetcorn, kidney beans and butter beans and mix well. Pour in the stock, give everything one final stir and let it simmer on the lowest heat for 30 minutes with the lid off. It is very important to let it simmer; it's like a fine wine that gets better with age.

3. After 30 minutes you'll notice that the soup is thickening as the beans soften. Stir through the coriander and the lime juice. Taste and add more salt or pepper if necessary.

4. Serve the soup sprinkled with more coriander.

IN THE BASKET

FAJITA SEASONING:
based on full jar

STOCK: based on full pack of cubes

Carrot and Coriander Soup

This traditional soup doesn't need any introduction: it's cheap, simple and really tasty. Who would have thought that something this flavoursome would be good for you? Also, if you believe the rumour that carrots help you see in the dark better, there are enough carrots in this soup to turn your eyes into night vision goggles! I've even included a pack of bake-at-home bread within the budget for good measure. Proper bargain!

VEGETARIAN

Ingredients

1 tbsp vegetable or olive oil

1 onion, chopped

2 garlic cloves, finely chopped

1 tsp ground coriander

1 large baking potato, roughly chopped

1kg carrots (from a budget range), roughly chopped

1 litre vegetable stock (made from a stock cube)

4 bake-at-home mini baguettes (1 pack of 4)

30g fresh coriander, roughly chopped, plus extra for serving

1 tbsp double cream, for serving

salt and pepper

Method

1. Put a pan on a medium heat and add the oil, then the onion. Let it soften for 3–4 minutes. Add the garlic and continue to cook for 2 minutes. Stir through the ground coriander and add the potato and carrots. Cover all the veggies in stock, put the lid on the pan and leave the soup to bubble away for 30 minutes (or until the potatoes and carrots are completely soft).

2. Towards the end of the 30 minutes, heat the oven to 180°C/160°C fan/gas mark 4, then put the baguettes into the oven and bake them until they are golden and crispy.

3. When the potatoes and carrots are soft, add the fresh coriander along with the stalks (there's plenty of flavour in the stalks so don't waste them).

4. Blend the soup to a consistency you like. You can use a handheld blender and blitz it in the pan, or you can transfer it to a food processor. When you're happy with the consistency, taste and add salt and pepper if needed.

5. Pour a couple of ladlefuls of soup into each bowl, add a pinch of black pepper, drizzle over some double cream and finally sprinkle more coriander on top.

IN THE BASKET

STOCK: based on full pack of cubes

DOUBLE CREAM: based on 150ml tub

Roasted Red Pepper Soup

This is such a tasty soup, which creates some strong flavour from very basic ingredients. Blistering and charring the peppers on a gas hob helps to bring out their incredible sweetness. But if you don't have a gas hob you can roast the peppers in the oven for 45 minutes instead. You can spice it up by adding some chilli flakes if you like or even add half a fresh chilli.

VEGETARIAN

Ingredients

4 red peppers
1 tbsp vegetable or olive oil, plus extra for frying croutons
1 onion, chopped
3 garlic cloves, finely chopped
400g tin chopped tomatoes
900ml vegetable stock (made from a stock cube)
1 crusty loaf, to serve
4 tbsp double cream, to serve
salt and pepper

Method

1. Start by blistering and charring the red peppers. Turn a gas burner to a high heat and use a pair of tongs to hold a pepper in the flame. Rotate the pepper every minute or so to hold a different side in the flame. You're aiming for a lot of black char marks on the pepper skin. It will take about 4–5 minutes to colour a pepper all over. You can char them one at a time on a single burner or turn on all four burners to char four peppers at once. Do what you feel comfortable with.

2. Once charred, place the peppers in a bowl, cover it with cling film and leave them for 5 minutes. This makes it easier to take off the skins. Remove the cling film and scrape as much of the charred skin from the peppers as you can. I use a butter knife for this.

3. Chop the peppers into chunks, removing the cores, stalks and seeds. Set them aside.

4. Put a large pan on a medium heat and add the oil and the onion with a pinch of salt. Let the onion soften for 4–5 minutes. Add the garlic and cook for a further minute.

5. Add the pepper chunks and tomatoes and give everything a good stir. Pour in the stock, put the lid on and let it simmer for 30 minutes.

6. Blend the soup to a consistency you like; you can use a food processor or a handheld blender for this.

7. Dice the bread, put a frying pan on a high heat, add a drop of oil and toss the cubes in the oil until crisp.

8. Serve the soup in wide bowls with a tablespoon of double cream drizzled over the top and the toasted bread cubes.

IN THE BASKET

STOCK: based on full pack of cubes

DOUBLE CREAM: based on 150ml tub

Tomato and Basil Soup with Garlic Bread

Forget the soup spoon and bowl – just grab a glass because you'll want to drink this by the pint. In fact scratch that; just get your swimming costume on and dive straight into it. This is a proper winter warmer and you will eat like a king or queen on a poor man's budget. This one can take some time to make, but we all know that good things come to those who wait.

VEGETARIAN

Ingredients

1 garlic bulb

vegetable or olive oil, for drizzling and frying

18 tomatoes, halved, cores removed

1 onion, finely chopped

1 carrot, finely chopped

1 celery stick, finely chopped

10 basil leaves, roughly chopped, plus extra for serving

1 litre vegetable stock (made from a stock cube)

1 crusty baguette

salt and pepper

Method

1. Preheat the oven to 180°C/160°C fan/gas mark 4.

2. Start by chopping off the top of the garlic bulb, exposing all the cloves. Put it on a piece of foil, drizzle over some oil and sprinkle over some salt and pepper. Wrap the garlic in the foil, place it in the centre of a baking tray and put it in the oven for 30 minutes.

3. After 30 minutes, add the tomatoes to the baking tray, flesh side up, drizzle over some oil and add some salt and pepper. Put the baking tray back into the oven for a further 30 minutes.

4. Remove the tray, unwrap the garlic and squeeze the flesh from the cloves. You'll be left with a mellow garlic paste.

5. Put a frying pan on a medium heat, add a drop of oil and the onion, carrot and celery. Be super patient with these veggies; let them soften and cook for at least 15 minutes.

6. When they are soft, add half the garlic paste to the pan and mix it through. Add the tomatoes and basil and cover everything with the stock. Put the lid on and let it bubble away for 15 minutes.

7. Blend the soup to a consistency you like; I prefer mine quite chunky (almost with the texture of a paste) but if you like it thinner that's also fine.

8. Make very simple garlic bread, by cutting the baguette in half lengthways. Spread the remaining garlic paste over the cut sides and toast the halves in a griddle pan.

9. Serve the soup in a bowl with a couple of basil leaves, some black pepper and the garlic bread for dipping.

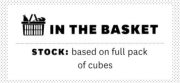

IN THE BASKET

STOCK: based on full pack of cubes

Chunky Chorizo Soup with Croutons

Who would have thought you could use chorizo in a budget dish? Well, believe it or not, you can. Yeah I'm as surprised as you – you have to use prepacked thinly-sliced chorizo but it really doesn't matter when you're chucking it into a soup! This is properly simple and really delivers on flavour. Make sure you've got some tissues handy because it's guaranteed to make you drool. Always start by chopping up your fresh ingredients so you have everything at your fingertips; you want to make life easy for yourself.

Ingredients

180g chorizo slices, finely chopped
1 red onion, finely chopped
3 garlic cloves, finely chopped
1 tsp paprika
400g tin chopped tomatoes
4 baking potatoes, chopped into 2cm chunks
125g tinned butter beans, drained
700ml chicken stock (made from a stock cube)
1 crusty cob loaf
vegetable or olive oil, for frying
handful of fresh parsley, finely chopped, plus extra for sprinkling
salt and pepper

Method

1. Put a large pan on a medium-high heat and add the chorizo. Let it cook for 2 minutes until it releases a lot of juices. Add the onion and cook for another 2 minutes, then the garlic and paprika and give everything a mix for about 30 seconds.
2. Add the tomatoes, potatoes and butter beans.
3. Give everything a good mix and then cover it in the stock and bring to a simmer. Put the lid on the pan and let it bubble away for about 30 minutes, or until the potatoes are nice and soft. You'll notice that as the potatoes soften the soup will thicken up.
4. While the soup is filling your house with incredible smells, make the croutons. Dice the cob, put a frying pan on a high heat, add a drop of oil and then toss the cob pieces in the oil until crisp. Put the croutons aside for later.
5. When the potatoes are soft, the soup is almost ready to serve. Give it a taste and add some salt and pepper. Stir through a handful of parsley.
6. Serve the soup topped with some croutons and another sprinkling of parsley.

IN THE BASKET

PAPRIKA: based on a full jar

STOCK: based on full pack of cubes

Knock-off French Onion Soup

If you know me you've probably gathered that elegance and I don't go in the same sentence. But let me tell you that I went elegant and sophisticated with this one! It's a knock-off French onion soup and you're going to absolutely love it! I'm probably going to get roasted for this but I top it with mozzarella instead of Gruyère; the reason is that mozzarella is miles cheaper – and you get some incredible cheese pulls with it too.

Ingredients

2 tbsp vegetable or olive oil
7 onions, thinly sliced
4 garlic cloves, finely chopped
1 heaped tbsp plain flour
4 tbsp Worcestershire sauce
1 tbsp fresh thyme leaves, plus extra for serving
950ml beef stock (made from a stock cube)
125g ball mozzarella
1 crusty roll
salt and pepper

Method

1. Put a pan on a low heat and add the oil followed by the onions. Take good care of the onions, moving them every couple of minutes to ensure that they do not burn. It will take 30 minutes to cook them until they caramelise. You want them to be golden brown.

2. Add the garlic and cook for a further minute, then stir through the flour and mix well until there are no lumps visible.

3. Add the Worcestershire sauce and thyme and mix well. Preheat the oven to 180°C/160°C fan/gas mark 4.

4. Pour in the stock, put the lid on the pan and allow the soup to simmer and bubble away on a low heat for 10 minutes.

5. After 10 minutes you'll notice that it has thickened and become wonderfully silky. Add some salt and pepper.

6. Divide the soup equally into 4 ovenproof bowls or dishes arranged on a baking tray (I have some miniature casserole dishes which make it look appealing).

7. Cut the crusty roll into 2cm chunks and place them on top of the soup. Break the ball of mozzarella into chunks and place them on top of the bread.

8. Put the baking tray in the oven for 10 minutes or until the cheese has melted and turned golden. Scatter a few thyme leaves on top and serve.

IN THE BASKET

FLOUR: based on 500g bag
WORCESTERSHIRE SAUCE: based on full bottle
STOCK: based on full pack of cubes

Broccoli and Cheddar Soup

I have a confession: I'm not a big fan of broccoli. But I do like this soup and can confirm that it tastes really nice – probably because there's cheese in it! We all know that cheese makes everything taste better. If you want to give this soup a bit of a kick you could add a few chilli flakes – tweak it to your taste and make it your own.

VEGETARIAN

Ingredients

1 tbsp vegetable or olive oil
2 onions, finely chopped
4 garlic cloves, finely chopped
2 baking potatoes, cut into 2cm chunks
1kg broccoli, florets removed and stalks peeled and cut into 2cm chunks
2 litres vegetable stock (made from a stock cube)
180g mature Cheddar cheese, plus extra to serve
salt and pepper

Method

1. Start by putting a large pan or Dutch oven on a low heat. Add the oil followed by the onions. Season with a pinch of salt and let the onions soften for 8–10 minutes. Don't brown or caramelise them, just soften them until they are translucent.
2. Add the garlic and cook for a further 2 minutes, then add the potato and the broccoli stalks to the pan along with the stock and bring to a simmer. Put the lid on and let it bubble away for 20 minutes, or until the potatoes and stalks are tender.
3. Add half the broccoli florets and continue to cook for 5 minutes.
4. Remove the pan from the heat and blend the contents until smooth. I use a handheld blender, but you can also use a food processor to blitz it in batches.
5. Return the pan to the heat and add the rest of the broccoli florets. Allow them to bubble away for 5 minutes.
6. Add the cheese and salt and pepper and mix well. When the cheese has melted the soup is ready. Sprinkle over more cheese and a dusting of black pepper to serve.

Curried Carrot Soup

What a beautiful winter warmer this one truly is. It's a great fusion of carrot soup and curry sauce and you will want to make it time and time again. You can tweak the heat to your liking; if you're a bit of a wuss when it comes to spice, then buy a mild korma curry powder and don't add much chilli (you can also deseed the chilli for a milder soup). If you want it at the other end of the scale, then use a hot curry powder and add a couple more chillies. You can use any type of bread you like; it works well with toasted crusty bread. If you want to take it up a level you can use naan bread, which goes down an absolute treat!

VEGAN

Ingredients

2 tbsp vegetable or olive oil
1 onion, chopped
1kg carrots (from a budget range), roughly chopped
½ chilli, finely chopped, plus slices to serve
4 garlic cloves, finely chopped
thumb-size piece of ginger, finely chopped
5 tbsp curry powder
600ml vegetable stock (made from a stock cube)
400ml coconut milk
2 naan breads, to serve
salt and pepper

Method

1. Put a large pot on a medium heat, add the oil and then the onion, carrots and chilli with some salt and pepper. Cook for 4–5 minutes until everything begins to soften.
2. Add the garlic and ginger and cook for a further 2 minutes, then add the curry powder and stir for a further minute.
3. Add the vegetable stock and coconut milk, mix well and put on the lid. Let the soup simmer on a low heat for 30 minutes until the carrots have completely softened.
4. Take the pan off the heat and either transfer to a food processor or use a handheld blender to blitz it to a consistency you like.
5. Return the pan to the heat to warm up the soup, tasting and adding more salt if necessary.
6. Ladle the soup into 4 bowls and serve with slices of chilli, a sprinkling of black pepper and warm naan or other bread of your choice.

IN THE BASKET

CURRY POWDER: based on full jar

STOCK: based on full pack of cubes

Spicy Noodle Soup

A very simple and super-quick noodle soup with only six ingredients! If you're feeling experimental it's an adaptable soup and you can easily add a few extras here and there to pimp it up a bit! There's a fantastic blend of ingredients in the store-bought red Thai curry paste, but you could also add some minced garlic, ginger, sliced chillies, beansprouts or even sugar snap peas or mangetout. Here's how to make the basic version (which is incredibly tasty with a spicy kick!)

VEGETARIAN

Ingredients

1 tbsp vegetable or olive oil

180g Thai red curry paste

400ml coconut milk

1.3 litres vegetable stock (made from a stock cube)

340g dried egg noodles

70g spring onions, finely sliced, to serve

squeeze of lime juice, to serve

salt and pepper

Method

1. Put a large pan on a medium heat and add the oil, then the curry paste and cook for 1 minute until fragrant. Pour in the coconut milk, mix it well with the curry paste and bring to a simmer.

2. Add the stock and the noodles. The soup may look a little thin at this stage but the noodles will soak up a lot of the liquid. Put the lid on and let it bubble away on a low heat for 4–5 minutes until the noodles are soft.

3. Season with salt and pepper, then add the spring onions and a squeeze of lime juice. Serve piping hot.

IN THE BASKET

STOCK: based on full pack of cubes

Memory Lane

Food from my Childhood

Toad in the Hole

Food like this takes me right back to when I was a kid. This British comfort food simply brings a smile to your face. Succulent sausages engulfed in a Yorkshire pudding batter are absolutely amazing! For this recipe I've gone to the trouble of including vegetables and an entire tub of gravy within the budget. I've chosen carrots and peas, but you can use any vegetables you like. It's a complete feast for under a fiver!

Ingredients

8 pork sausages
6 tbsp vegetable oil
250g plain flour
1 tsp salt
4 medium eggs
180ml milk
4 carrots, to serve
320g frozen peas, to serve
600ml gravy, to serve

Method

1. Preheat the oven to 190°C/170°C fan/gas mark 5. Put the sausages in a baking dish (about 25 x 18cm). Add the vegetable oil and bake the sausages in the oven for 15 minutes.

2. Put the flour and salt into a mixing bowl and crack the eggs into a separate bowl, then whisk them until the yolks and whites are combined.

3. Add the eggs to the flour and give them a good stir; this will start to bring the flour together. Add the milk gradually, mixing all the time. The mixture will eventually form a silky batter.

4. For this next part you need to be quick. Take the sausages out of the oven and tip the batter all over them. Make sure the batter completely covers the bottom of the baking dish and swiftly put the dish back in the oven for 15 minutes. If you're not quick, the hot vegetable oil will cool down and you will not get a good rise on the Yorkshire pudding batter.

5. After 15 minutes, the batter should have risen nicely and completely swallowed up the sausages. Now put your vegetables on to boil and prepare the gravy.

6. Serve with the vegetables and some thick gravy.

IN THE BASKET

FLOUR: based on 1.5kg bag

EGGS: based on box of 6

MILK: based on 1 pint bottle

PEAS: based on 900g bag

Cheese and Potato Pie

This is one of those meals where you seem to throw random ingredients together and hope for the best – and although there's some truth in that, it absolutely works! Baked beans and hot dogs? Yeah, just chuck them in. Some bacon as well? Yeah, dash that in too. Cheese in the mash? Use the entire block! You only live once don't you?

Ingredients

4 large baking potatoes, cut into 2cm chunks
8 slices bacon, chopped
1 onion, finely chopped
1 garlic clove, chopped
4 hot dogs, cut into 2cm pieces
2 x 400g tins baked beans (from a budget range)
200g Cheddar cheese, grated
salt and pepper

Method

1. Fill a pan with cold water and add about a teaspoon of salt. Put in the potatoes, bring them to the boil and simmer them until they're soft.

2. While the potatoes cook, put a frying pan on a medium-high heat and add the bacon (you don't need oil as the bacon will release fat as it cooks). Cook the bacon until it's crispy, then take it out of the pan and set it aside.

3. Put the onion in the frying pan and let it soften in the leftover bacon fat for 2–3 minutes. Add the garlic and cook for a further 2 minutes. Preheat the oven to 180°C/160°C fan/gas mark 4.

4. Return the bacon to the pan and add the hot dogs, then the beans and some black pepper and give everything a good mix. Let it bubble away for 2–3 minutes.

5. While it's bubbling divide the grated cheese into two piles.

6. Drain the potatoes and mash them, ensuring that there are as few lumps as possible. Be generous with the salt and pepper. Mash half the cheese into the potato until it is melted and combined.

7. Transfer the bean and hot dog mixture to a baking dish and layer the mashed cheesy potato on top in the style of a cottage pie. Smooth the top of the potato and make sure that you can't see any beans.

8. Sprinkle the rest of the cheese over the top of the potato.

9. Bake in the oven for 20 minutes until the cheese is golden on top.

IN THE BASKET

SAUSAGES: based on 400g tin

Cottage Pie

Who would have thought it possible to make a cottage pie for under a fiver? Well it really is, believe it or not! This is extremely basic as I've stripped it back to very humble ingredients. Believe me when I say that it does what it says on the tin and is an absolute treat in the winter months – especially when the bank balance is looking pretty bleak towards the end of January!

Ingredients

1 tbsp vegetable or olive oil

1 onion, finely chopped

1 carrot, finely chopped

1 celery stick, finely chopped

3 garlic cloves, finely chopped

3 rosemary sprigs

500g minced beef

1 tbsp tomato purée

500ml beef stock (made from a stock cube)

700g potatoes, chopped into 2cm pieces

salt and pepper

Method

1. Put a pan on a medium heat and add the oil, onion, carrot and celery and cook them for 10 minutes until the veggies are nice and soft.

2. Add the garlic and rosemary and cook for a further 2 minutes. Add the mince and break it up into small pieces with the back of a wooden spoon; you don't want any big lumps of meat. Add salt and pepper to taste and cook until the meat is nice and brown.

3. Preheat the oven to 180°C/160°C fan/gas mark 4.

4. Add the tomato purée to the mince and stir it through until it is well combined with the meat and veggies. Now add the beef stock. I start by adding about 300ml or just enough to cover the meat. Save the rest of the stock to top up the pan while it's simmering. Let it simmer for 15–20 minutes.

5. Fill a pan with cold water and add salt. Put in the potatoes and bring them to a boil. Cook until the potatoes are soft, then drain.

6. Season the potatoes generously with salt and pepper and mash them. Try to make the mash as smooth as possible (you can add butter, milk, cream or cheese if you have any in the fridge, although they are not included in this budget recipe).

7. When the stock in the mince pan has reduced and thickened; transfer the contents to a baking dish. Top the mince with the mashed potato and run a fork over the top to make a pattern (you can top with some cheese if you have some in the fridge).

8. Bake in the oven for 30 minutes or until the top is a golden colour. You'll notice that the potato gets a thin layer of crispiness as it cooks. You're now ready to serve and enjoy.

IN THE BASKET

TOMATO PUREE: based on 200g tube

STOCK: based on full pack of cubes

Beef Hot Pot

It's almost unbelievable how far you can make a fiver stretch when you put your mind to it. This is a great example of how to turn the most basic and humble ingredients into a proper people pleaser. Put this bad boy in the centre of the table fresh out of the oven and just watch people's faces light up. When it's piled on your plate it won't win any awards for the best-looking dish, but it will roll back the years and take you back to when you were a kid in the middle of winter. I always used to eat this when I was growing up; it was a staple in my house. Give it a go and it could become a regular on your shopping list!

Ingredients

1 tbsp vegetable or olive oil, plus extra for brushing

500g minced beef (20% fat)

2 onions, finely chopped

2 carrots, diced

1 tbsp flour (optional)

1 tsp fresh thyme leaves, plus extra to serve

100g frozen peas

500ml beef stock (made from a stock cube)

1 heaped tbsp horseradish sauce

4 baking potatoes, sliced to the thickness of a £1 coin

salt and pepper

Method

1. Preheat the oven to 180°C/160°C fan/gas mark 4.
2. Put a pan on a high heat and add a tablespoon of oil. Add the mince and break it up with the back of a wooden spoon, making sure there are no big lumps. Add a generous amount of salt and pepper (there's nothing worse than under-seasoned meat!). Brown the meat, then set it aside for later.
3. Use the same pan to cook the onions and let them soften for at least 5 minutes before adding the carrots. Return the mince to the pan and give everything a mix.
4. Add the flour, if using. I recommend it to help thicken the sauce as it cooks. Stir it through the mixture, ensuring that there are no lumps. Add the thyme and the peas and stir again.
5. Pour in the beef stock and add the horseradish sauce, then let it bubble away for 3–4 minutes.
6. Transfer the mince mixture into a baking dish (I use a 25 x 18cm dish) and layer the potatoes on top so they overlap slightly. This looks pretty and stops them sinking too much into the beef.
7. Brush the potatoes lightly with oil and bake in the oven for 1 hour.
8. Take out the baking dish and sprinkle over a few thyme leaves, then put it under a hot grill for 5 minutes to crisp up the potatoes. You're now ready to serve.

IN THE BASKET

PEAS: based on 850g bag

STOCK: based on full pack of cubes

HORSERADISH SAUCE: based on full jar

Bubble and Squeak

This is such an indulgent and comforting way of using up leftover veggies, whether they are the odds and sods in your fridge on the verge of going out of date or the leftover cooked veg from a roast dinner. It's also easy to cook the veggies from scratch! This recipe is versatile and works with pretty much any veg. I've based it on potatoes, carrots, swede and cabbage, but you can use whatever you have (mashed-up sprouts, parsnips or even cauliflower). I serve mine with a runny-yolk fried egg and it's an absolute treat. I have many happy memories of eating it. If you struggle to get your kids to eat veg, then give it a try; it will be difficult for them to tell which vegetables are in it!

Ingredients

700g cooked potatoes
250g cooked swede
400g cooked carrots
2 tbsp vegetable or olive oil
5 slices of bacon, chopped into
   small pieces
1 leek, finely sliced
170g Savoy cabbage, finely sliced
6 eggs, plus an extra yolk
2 knobs of butter (optional)
salt and pepper

Method

1. Mash the potatoes, carrots and swede, season generously with salt and pepper and in a large mixing bowl, then set aside.

2. Put a frying pan on a high heat and add a tablespoon of oil, then the bacon. Cook for 2–3 minutes until the bacon begins to crisp. Then add the leek and cabbage and cook for a further 2 minutes. You want a bit of colour on these. Transfer the bacon, leek and cabbage into the mixing bowl and mix well with the potatoes, carrots and swede.

3. Allow everything to cool completely, then add an egg yolk to the mixing bowl and stir it through.

4. Shape the mixture into patties for pan frying. You can make them as big or small as you like – I make mine about 2cm thick and 12cm in diameter. Try and compress them as much as you can so they don't break up when cooking.

5. Put a large frying pan on a medium heat and add a tablespoon of oil. Carefully lay the patties in the pan and cook for 2 minutes on each side until they are golden and crispy. If you have some butter in your fridge add a couple of small pieces to the pan to make the patties more golden. Once they're cooked take them out and divide them between 6 plates.

6. Use the same pan to fry the eggs, cooking them so they have beautifully runny yolks. Lay a fried egg on top of each patty, add a crack of black pepper and serve.

Posh Beans on Toast

This recipe is a far cry from the beans on toast I had when I was growing up. When I was younger we had the usual tinned baked beans on a slice of toasted white bread, with a bit of cheese if we were lucky. We would eat this a couple of times a week and I used to absolutely love it. So I thought I'd turn humble beans on toast into a celebration of my childhood. I know what you're thinking: 'But Mitch that defeats the idea of cooking a budget meal when I can buy a couple of cheap tins of baked beans and a 70p loaf of bread!' You're right. But this is still an incredibly cheap meal for the quantity of food you need to buy so don't knock it until you try it. It has bacon in it and we all know that bacon makes everything better.

Ingredients

1 tbsp vegetable or olive oil

8 slices of bacon, chopped into small pieces

½ onion, finely chopped

3 garlic cloves, finely chopped

2 x 400g tins chopped tomatoes

2 x 400g tins haricot beans, drained

1 tbsp sugar

1 bloomer loaf

2 spring onions, green ends sliced, to serve

salt and pepper

Method

1. Put a pan on a medium heat and add the oil, then the bacon pieces. Cook them for 2–3 minutes until coloured.

2. Add the onion and continue to cook for 2 minutes, then the garlic and cook for 1 more minute. By this point the bacon should be nice and crispy.

3. Add the tomatoes, followed by the beans and mix well. Fill one of the empty tins half full with water and add that too. Stir in the sugar and add salt and pepper to taste.

4. Put on the lid, turn down the heat to low and let everything simmer and bubble away for an hour. Check on it every 10 minutes or so to ensure that nothing is sticking to the bottom of the pan.

5. After an hour take the lid off and allow the mixture to bubble away for a further 15 minutes to thicken.

6. Cut thick slices from the loaf and toast them to your liking. I put mine in a griddle pan because I like charred bars across the slices, but you can also use a toaster or put them under the grill.

7. Taste the beans and add more salt and pepper if needed (or sugar if you want them a little sweeter). Spoon the beans over the toasted bread and serve with the spring onions on top.

IN THE BASKET

SUGAR: based on 500g bag

Chicken Stew

It isn't elegant and it isn't pretty, but you can bet that this was one of my favourite winter meals as a kid. With minimal effort you can create an absolute slammer of a meal to feed your family – it's so cheap and so easy to make! The veggies I use are potatoes, carrots and leeks; but you can chop and change to any vegetables you prefer.

Ingredients

1kg chicken drumsticks

2 tbsp vegetable or olive oil

4 baking potatoes, cut into 3cm chunks

500g carrots, cut into 3cm chunks

2 tbsp tomato purée

1 litre chicken stock (made from a stock cube)

1 tbsp ready-made English mustard

1 leek, roughly chopped

25g fresh parsley, finely chopped (optional)

salt and pepper

Method

1. Start by seasoning the drumsticks with a generous amount of salt and pepper. Rub them into the meat, ensuring that every piece has some seasoning.
2. Put a large casserole pot or Dutch oven on a high heat, add the oil and then add the drumsticks. Sear them on all sides until golden brown.
3. Add the potatoes and carrots along with the tomato purée. Give everything a good mix for 1 minute, then add the stock and mustard and mix well again. Put on the lid, turn the heat downto low and simmer for 25 minutes.
4. After 25 minutes the meat should be falling off the bone. At this point add the leek, replace the lid and simmer for a further 5 minutes.
5. Take off the lid and simmer for another 5 minutes to reduce and thicken the sauce. As the potatoes soften they will help to thicken the sauce too.
6. Stir through the parsley, if using, and adjust the salt and pepper to taste. Give it one final mix and serve.

IN THE BASKET

TOMATO PUREE: based on 200g tube

MUSTARD: based on 200g jar

STOCK: based on full pack of cubes

Sausage Casserole

If you love a bit of sausage, then this is definitely one for you; it's an absolute classic and I reckon I must have eaten this at least once a week when I was a kid growing up. This dish brings back a lot of memories and I can honestly say that even at this point in my life, it's still one of my favourite home comfort meals. You never forget those childhood flavours.

Ingredients

1 tbsp vegetable or olive oil
8 pork sausages
1 onion (from a budget range), sliced
2 garlic cloves, finely chopped
3 baking potatoes, chopped into 4cm chunks
4 carrots, chopped into 4cm chunks
1 tbsp tomato purée
1 heaped tbsp plain flour
1 litre chicken stock (made from a stock cube)
1 tbsp ready-made English mustard
400g tin butter beans, drained
small bunch of fresh parsley, chopped, to serve (optional)
salt and pepper

Method

1. Heat a pan on a high heat and add the oil, then the sausages. Brown them all over, then take them out and put them to one side. It doesn't matter if they aren't cooked all the way through because you will finish cooking them later on.

2. Turn down the heat to medium, add the onion and allow it to soften for 5 minutes while constantly moving it around the pan. Add the garlic, potatoes and carrots and stir for 2 minutes. Then add the tomato purée and stir through. Add the flour and mix it in thoroughly, ensuring that no big lumps remain.

3. Cover everything in the stock, add the mustard and give it all another stir.

4. Put the lid on the pan and let it simmer for 20 minutes, or until the potatoes and carrots begin to soften.

5. Return the sausages to the pan along with the butter beans. Bring the casserole back to the boil and let it bubble away for a further 7–8 minutes on a low heat.

6. Stir through the parsley and serve.

IN THE BASKET

TOMATO PUREE: based on 200g tube

FLOUR: based on 500g bag

STOCK: based on full pack of cubes

MUSTARD: based on 200g jar

Roast Chicken Dinner

When I was growing up a traditional Sunday roast dinner was a staple in many British households. Every Sunday I had a roast dinner without fail – and it was always something to look forward to. I've stripped back and simplified the traditional roast to its bare bones here, but it will still be delicious! You will find it hard to believe that the cost of this entire meal was £4.63 (at the time of writing) and it gives you four generous portions of food. Cooking a roast dinner doesn't need to be stressful or hard work; with a bit of planning it can be very straightforward. The main thing is to pay attention to your timings. It's no good boiling veg at the same time as you're putting roast potatoes in the oven – that way you end up with soggy veg and undercooked spuds! Read on for a beginners' guide to cooking a budget roast dinner.

Ingredients

4 baking potatoes, cut into 2–3cm pieces
4–5 tbsp vegetable or olive oil
1 onion, roughly chopped
1kg carrots (from a budget range) roughly chopped
1 garlic bulb, cloves crushed in their skins
1kg chicken legs (4–5 legs)
2 tbsp plain flour
800ml chicken stock (made from a stock cube)
220g green beans (from a budget range)
salt and pepper

Method

1. Preheat the oven to 200°C/180°C fan/gas mark 6.
2. Fill a pan with cold water and add a pinch of salt followed by the potatoes. Bring the water to a simmer and cook the potatoes for 10 minutes. They are done when you can pierce them easily with a fork.
3. Drain the potatoes and toss them gently to roughen the edges (this helps the outsides to crisp). Season generously with salt and pepper and let them dry completely in the colander.
4. While the potatoes are drying, heat a baking tray with the oil in the oven for 15 minutes.
5. When the oil is hot carefully place the dry potatoes on the baking tray (they will sizzle slightly). Roast them in the oven for 30 minutes.
6. Put the onion, 3 carrots and 2 garlic cloves in a deep baking tray. Score the chicken legs to the bone and lay them on top. Season generously with salt and pepper and roast everything in the oven for 1 hour.
7. After 30 minutes take the potatoes out of the oven, flip them over and add the remaining garlic cloves (I leave them in their skins to prevent them burning). Put the potatoes back in the oven for 45 minutes.

8. When the chicken legs are cooked, remove them from the baking tray and set them aside under some foil to keep warm.

9. To make the gravy put the chicken baking tray on a medium heat and cover the onions and carrots in the flour. Stir until there are no big lumps and then pour in the stock. Bring it to a simmer and let it bubble away and reduce until thick.

10. While the gravy is bubbling away put the remaining carrots to boil in salted water until they are cooked to your liking (I like mine with a crunch, but some people like them softer). When the carrots are almost done, add the green beans to the pan (they will take 3–4 minutes at most).

11. By this stage the chicken gravy should be nice and thick; pass it through a sieve and pour it into a gravy boat or jug.

12. Take the roast potatoes out of the oven and plate up the carrots, green beans and chicken legs. Serve with the gravy.

🗑 **IN THE BASKET**

FLOUR: based on 500g bag

STOCK: based on full pack of cubes

Slow Cooker Chicken Curry

I remember the times as a kid when I'd come in from school and the slow cooker was on in the kitchen. I knew that 90 per cent of the time it would contain a bland stew or casserole that would turn out to be completely overcooked. This recipe is one of the 10 per cent of meals that were delicious – trust me. This one will make your family excited to see that the slow cooker is on when they arrive home! The smell that hits you when you open the front door is incredible. There is so much flavour in this curry and it needs very little prep. It's a gem of a recipe for the winter months. I recommend prepping it the night before so you can throw it together the following morning and then go about your busy day. That will also allow it to marinate overnight for maximum flavour!

Ingredients

1kg chicken legs, skinned
1 onion, finely chopped
1 garlic bulb, finely chopped
2 chillies (1 finely chopped and
   1 left whole)
thumb-sized piece of ginger
   (about 10g), finely chopped
10g fresh coriander leaves and
   stalks, finely chopped
2 tbsp vegetable or olive oil
5 tbsp curry powder
400g tin chopped tomatoes
salt and pepper

Method

1. Score the chicken pieces a few times, cutting through the flesh to the bone to allow all the flavours to penetrate. Put them into a bowl along with the onion, garlic, chillies (deseeded for a milder curry), ginger and coriander stalks. Add the oil along with 4 tablespoons of curry powder and salt and pepper to taste.

2. Use your hands to massage all the seasoning and other ingredients into the chicken pieces. Cover the bowl in cling film and put it in the fridge to marinate. The longer you leave it the better the flavour, but it's also fine to start cooking straight away.

3. When you're ready to cook put a pan on a high heat until it's screaming hot and sear the chicken legs for 2 minutes on each side until they're brown. Try not to add too many onion and garlic pieces to the hot pan as they will burn and taste bitter.

4. Put the chicken pieces into the slow cooker along with the marinated onions, garlic, chillies and ginger. Add the tomatoes, 100ml water, 1 tablespoon curry powder and salt and pepper to taste.

5. Give everything a mix, set the slow cooker to low, put on the lid and leave it to cook for 8 hours. You are now free to go about your day. When you check 8 hours later, you'll notice that the chicken is falling off the bone. Sprinkle with the coriander leaves and serve.

Method if you don't own a slow cooker

1. Marinate the meat by following the first 2 steps opposite.
2. Put a large pan with a lid or a Dutch oven on a high heat and sear
    the chicken as opposite for 2 minutes on each side. When the meat
    is a golden colour, turn down the heat to medium and add the
    onion, garlic, ginger and chilli from the marinating bowl. Continue to
    cook for 2 minutes. Keep everything moving as you don't want the
    garlic to burn or it will turn bitter.
3. Add the tomatoes, 400ml water and 1 tablespoon curry powder (for
    more flavour). Give it all a stir. You can also add a whole chilli if you
    like a little extra spice.
4. Put on the lid and simmer for 45 minutes. Keep your eye on the pan
    and add a drop more water when required. Stir regularly to ensure
    that nothing sticks to the bottom (especially if using a Dutch oven).
5. Take the lid off for the final 10 minutes and allow it to continue to
    bubble away on a low heat to thicken the sauce. Ideally the meat
    should be falling off the bone and be nice and tender.
6. Finish with a sprinkling of coriander leaves and serve.

IN THE BASKET

CURRY POWDER: based on
full jar

Mushroom Stroganoff with Jacket Spuds

Let's smother some jacket potatoes in a budget homemade mushroom stroganoff! When the weather starts to get cold, this recipe offers a bit of comforting indulgence. Jacket spuds were a staple in my house when I was growing up: they're cheap, versatile and super filling. I used to have all sorts on them – curry, cheesy beans, chilli con carne, tuna and sweetcorn – the list is endless. It's always nice to think outside the box with a spud filling or topping. That's where this beauty comes in! It's not a traditional stroganoff, but it's a fantastic tasting variation within a budget. Have a go and I'm sure you'll want to make it again and again.

VEGETARIAN

Ingredients

4 baking potatoes
1 tbsp vegetable or olive oil
1 onion, finely chopped
400g mushrooms (from a budget range), cut into chunks
4 garlic cloves, finely chopped
1 tsp paprika
1 tbsp flour
400ml vegetable stock (made from a stock cube)
1 heaped tbsp sour cream
1 tbsp own-brand Dijon or French mustard
handful of fresh parsley, finely chopped, plus extra to serve
salt and pepper

IN THE BASKET

PAPRIKA: based on full jar
STOCK: based on full pack of cubes
SOUR CREAM: based on 150ml tub
MUSTARD: based on 200g jar

Method

1. Preheat the oven to 180°C/160°C fan/gas mark 4. Wrap the potatoes separately in foil and put them in the oven for 1 hour 20 minutes.

2. About 15 minutes before the spuds are due to come out of the oven put a frying pan on a medium heat and add the oil. Add the onion and cook for 3–4 minutes until soft. Keep moving the onions around the pan to prevent them burning.

3. Add the mushrooms, season with salt and pepper and cook them for 3–4 minutes. This may seem a lot of mushrooms but they shrink as they cook. Add the garlic and cook for a further minute, then add the paprika and stir through.

4. Add the flour and stir it through, ensuring that there are no big lumps. Pour in the stock and let the sauce simmer and reduce for 5 minutes. It will begin to thicken.

5. Stir through the sour cream and mustard and let the mixture bubble away for another minute. Add the parsley to finish.

6. By this point the potatoes will be nice and soft so take them out of the oven, cut them in half and ladle the mushroom stroganoff over them. Finish with another sprinkling of fresh parsley.

Bangers and Mash with Onion Gravy

Surely bangers and mash has to be ranked as Britain's number one comfort food? Are you even British if you've never eaten it? I have to set the scene with this one. Picture a day when it's freezing outside (and I'm talking –3°C). It's the middle of January, properly windy and already pitch black on your way home from work. You're craving a hot, comforting and wholesome meal and all of a sudden you remember you have sausages, potatoes and onions in the kitchen. Thank me later.

Ingredients

1 tbsp vegetable or olive oil

8 pork sausages

4 tbsp baking spread

2 onions (or 5 from a budget range), thinly sliced

8 baking potatoes, chopped into 2cm chunks

1 tbsp flour

6 thyme sprigs

600ml beef stock (made from a stock cube)

small bunch of fresh parsley (optional), finely chopped, plus extra to serve

salt and pepper

Method

1. Put a frying pan on a high heat, add the oil and then put the sausages in the pan. Brown them evenly all over. It doesn't matter if the sausages are not completely cooked; you just need to colour them at this point. Take them out of the pan and set them aside for later.

2. Turn the heat down to low and put in 1 tablespoon of the spread and the onions. It's important to be patient with the onions; it will take 30 minutes to caramelise them. Move them around the pan to prevent them sticking and burning.

3. While the onions are softening, fill a saucepan with cold water, add salt and put the potatoes in the water. Bring them to a boil and simmer until soft.

4. When the onions have softened and become caramelised add the flour and mix well. Add some salt and pepper and the thyme sprigs. Cover the onions in the stock and give everything another stir.

5. Bring the mixture to a simmer and let it bubble away for 20 minutes. The stock will thicken and create a rich gravy.

6. Remove the thyme from the pan and return the sausages. Let the mixture bubble away for a further 5 minutes to finish cooking the sausages.

7. Drain the potatoes, season generously with salt and pepper and mix in 3 tablespoons of the spread. Mash the potatoes as well as you can (if you want them extra smooth you can pass them through a sieve). Mix through the parsley.

8. Place a bed of mash on each plate with two sausages on top and spoon over the rich onion gravy. Be generous with it; you only live once. Sprinkle over some more parsley for a finishing touch. I can smell it as I write this. Absolutely heavenly.

🗑 IN THE BASKET

BAKING SPREAD: based on 500g tub

FLOUR: based on 1kg bag

STOCK: based on full pack of cubes

Pasta

Tuna Pasta Bake

Hot tuna has always divided opinion, but I think this recipe will convince anyone that there's a place for hot tuna in their lives. My kids are properly fussy when it comes to dinner – where pasta's concerned they will only eat it completely plain. That was until I cooked them this tuna pasta bake; they now eat pasta with something on it! So if it works on my kids, I'd like to suggest that it will convince yours too. Have a go and you won't regret it, I promise – it has to be worth a try for a fiver!

Ingredients

400g penne (from a budget range)
1 tbsp vegetable or olive oil
1 onion (from a budget range),
    finely chopped
3 garlic cloves, finely chopped
400g tin chopped tomatoes
2 x 120g tins tuna in spring water,
    drained
250g grated mozzarella
salt and pepper

Method

1. Begin by preheating the oven to 180°C/160°C fan/gas mark 4. Bring a large pan of salted water to the boil and add the penne. Cook until tender, then drain, reserving some of the cooking water.

2. Put another pan on a medium heat and add the oil and the onion. Allow it to soften for 3–4 minutes, then add the garlic and continue to cook for 2 minutes.

3. Add the tomatoes and tuna and give everything a stir. Add a ladle of pasta water to loosen the sauce and make it more liquid.

4. Spoon in the cooked pasta and mix it thoroughly with the tomatoes and tuna. Add a generous handful of mozzarella along with salt and pepper to taste and stir once more.

5. Transfer it all to a baking dish and top with the rest of the cheese. Be generous with the cheese! If you have some ready-salted crisps in your cupboard you can sprinkle some crushed crisps on top of the cheese to add a little crunch.

6. Bake in the oven for 20 minutes until the cheese topping is melted and golden.

IN THE BASKET

PASTA: based on 500g bag

Spaghetti and Meatballs

I'm really stretching the budget with this one, but managed to buy all of the ingredients for this recipe for bang on a fiver. No ready-made meatballs or jarred sauces here – we're making everything from scratch because it tastes so much better! Properly juicy meatballs in a rich homemade tomato and basil sauce smothered over spaghetti. Sounds heavenly doesn't it? I managed to make 20 meatballs with these quantities but you can make them as big or small as you like!

Ingredients

3 tbsp olive or vegetable oil

2 onions – 1 finely sliced and 1 grated

5 garlic cloves, finely chopped

2 x 400g tins tomatoes

8–10 fresh basil leaves, plus extra to serve

500g minced beef (20% fat)

1 tbsp Italian herb seasoning

½ slice of bread, blitzed into breadcrumbs

400g spaghetti (own brand)

salt and pepper

Method

1. Start by making the tomato sauce; put a large pan on a medium heat, add a tablespoon of the oil and the sliced onion and cook for 3–4 minutes until softened. Keep moving the onion; don't allow it to burn and go bitter.

2. Add 2 of the garlic cloves and continue to cook for 1 minute. Tip in the tomatoes, then half fill one tin with water and tip that in too.

3. Add the basil leaves, plus salt and pepper to taste. Give everything a good mix and reduce the heat to the lowest setting, then let it simmer for 30 minutes. It's important to let the sauce simmer so that all the flavours develop and become richer. Keep your eye on it and add a splash more water if it starts to look too thick.

4. Put the mince, the grated onion (which should have a paste-like texture), the remaining 3 garlic cloves, the mixed herbs, the breadcrumbs, 1 tablespoon of the oil and salt and pepper into a mixing bowl. Use your hands to squeeze everything together so it is nicely combined.

5. Shape the mixture into meatballs by rolling them in your hands. It will make between 15 and 20 depending on how big you make them.

6. Put a frying pan on a high heat, add the remaining oil and carefully place the meatballs in the pan. You need to sear the meatballs until they are brown. It doesn't matter whether they are completely cooked through as you will finish cooking them later. When all the meatballs are coloured, take them out of the pan, set them aside and wipe the pan.

7. Blend the tomato sauce to a consistency you like. I blitz mine so there are no chunks (I don't want my kids knowing that there are onions in it).
8. Pour the sauce into the clean pan and bring it to a simmer. Put the meatballs into the sauce, put the lid on and let them bubble away for 10 minutes.
9. Put a large pan of salted water on to boil and add the spaghetti once it is boiling.
10. When the spaghetti is cooked, drain it and assemble everything. Put a bed of spaghetti under the meatballs, then spoon over the tomato sauce. Serve with some small fresh basil leaves on top.

🧺 IN THE BASKET

ITALIAN HERBS: based on full jar

BREAD: based on 800g loaf

SPAGHETTI: based on 1kg pack

Mac and Cheese

You need to take out a bank loan these days to buy a packet of butter so I'm going to cheat a bit and use baking block. Don't worry though, it makes absolutely no difference to the finished dish! It's still rich, cheesy, indulgent and properly comforting! This is a very basic mac and cheese and my kids go wild for it. Who doesn't like pasta with a gooey cheese sauce? I'm getting hungry just thinking about it. If you want to experiment and increase your budget, then you could bake it with breadcrumbs on top or even add bacon bits.

VEGETARIAN

Ingredients

500g macaroni
50g baking block
50g plain flour
568ml (1 pint) milk
100g Cheddar cheese, grated, plus
   extra for sprinkling on top
salt and pepper

Method

1. Bring a large pan of salted water to the boil, add the macaroni and cook until tender, then drain.

2. When the macaroni is almost cooked, put another large pan on a medium heat and add the baking block. When it has melted, add the flour and give it a stir.

3. Gradually add the milk, stirring continuously. Keep adding milk, little by little, until there are no lumps of flour. Bring the sauce to a simmer, continuing to stir. You'll notice it begin to thicken.

4. While the sauce is simmering, add the cheese and salt and pepper to taste. Give the sauce a good mix while the cheese is melting.

5. Spoon the cooked macaroni into the sauce and stir it thoroughly. Transfer everything into a large, shallow baking dish and top with more cheese (as much or as little as you like!). I love a golden top so I'm generous with the cheese.

6. Put the baking dish under a hot grill until the cheese has melted and become golden. You're now ready to serve.

IN THE BASKET

PASTA: based on 500g bag

BAKING BLOCK: based on 500g tub

FLOUR: based on 500g bag

MILK: based on 1 pint bottle

CHEESE: based on 220g pack

Chicken Fajita Pasta

This is the pasta combination you didn't know you needed in your life until now – a properly elite combination that you will absolutely love! For this recipe I've used chicken drumsticks to keep the cost down, but if you want to increase your budget, then you can use chicken breasts instead. It's incredibly simple and you can throw this one together super quickly after work.

Ingredients

1kg chicken drumsticks, meat removed and cut into bite-sized pieces
35g fajita seasoning
400g rigatoni
1 tbsp vegetable or olive oil
1 red onion, sliced
1 yellow or orange pepper, sliced
3 garlic cloves, finely chopped
400g tin chopped tomatoes
squeeze lime juice, to serve
salt and pepper

Method

1. Put the meat into a bowl and cover it with half the fajita seasoning plus some salt and pepper. Use your hands to rub the spices into the meat and make sure every piece is seasoned.

2. Fill a large saucepan with water, salt it and bring it to the boil. Add the pasta and cook until tender, then drain, reserving some of the cooking liquid.

3. Put a large frying pan on a high heat until it's screaming hot, then add a tablespoon of oil and the chicken chunks. Cook for about 5 minutes until they are coloured, but avoid moving them around too much. When the chicken pieces are cooked through, take them out of the pan and set aside.

4. Lower the heat to medium and add the onion and pepper. Cook them for 2 minutes. Add the garlic, along with the remaining half of the fajita seasoning, and cook for a further minute. Add the tinned tomatoes along with half a ladle of pasta water and let everything simmer for 2 minutes.

5. Spoon the cooked pasta into the frying pan and mix it through. Return the cooked chicken and add a squeeze of lime juice. Taste and add more salt and pepper if necessary, then serve.

IN THE BASKET

FAJITA SEASONING: based on full jar

PASTA: based on 500g bag

Pea and Mint Tagliatelle

Don't be put off by the glow-in-the-dark green colour of this dish! This is such a fresh and satisfying pasta dish and perfect for the summer! It's very quick to make and if you have salt and pepper in your cupboard you can feed four people for £4.47 (at the time of writing). I find this recipe is a good way to get your kids to eat some vegetables. Once the peas are blended they won't have a clue what they're eating. I tell my son it's Incredible Hulk pasta and he wolfs it down!

VEGETARIAN

Ingredients

600g frozen peas
400g tagliatelle
15g fresh mint leaves, plus extra to serve
150g cream cheese
juice of 1 lemon, plus lemon slices to serve
Parmesan cheese, grated, to serve
salt and pepper

Method

1. Put the peas in a bowl or saucepan and soak them in boiling water for 5 minutes.
2. Bring a large saucepan of salted water to the boil. Add the tagliatelle and cook it until tender, then drain.
3. Drain the peas, return them to the bowl or saucepan and add the mint leaves, cheese, 200ml cold water, a generous amount of salt and pepper and half the lemon juice. Use a handheld blender or liquidiser to blitz the sauce until it's smooth.
4. Put another large pan on a low heat and tip in the blended pea and mint mixture. When it begins to bubble, start to add the cooked tagliatelle.
5. Mix the pasta through the sauce and taste it, adding more salt or lemon juice if necessary.
6. Plate up the pasta and serve it with a dusting of Parmesan on top, lemon slices on the side and a mint leaf in the middle.

🧺 IN THE BASKET

PEAS: based on 850g bag
PASTA: based on 500g bag
CREAM CHEESE: based on 200g tub
PARMESAN: based on 60g pack

Pesto Penne

This recipe involves buying just 6 ingredients and anybody can make it, regardless of cooking ability. There is no shame in using store-bought jarred pesto – it's quicker and so much easier! Having said that, if you want to be fancy then you are more than welcome to have a crack at making your own pesto. As we're on a budget a quid jar is fine for this. In some ways this is an elegant dish and I believe that if you cooked this for your partner on a date night you would be very likely to blow their mind. Save it for Valentine's day and thank me later.

VEGETARIAN

Ingredients

400g penne
1 tbsp olive oil
4 garlic cloves, finely chopped
300g cherry tomatoes, halved
190g jar green pesto
40g Parmesan, grated, plus extra
   to serve
20g (a handful) fresh parsley, finely
   chopped
salt and pepper

Method

1. Bring a large saucepan of salted water to the boil. Add the penne and cook until tender, then drain, reserving some of the cooking water.

2. Put a separate pan on a low heat and add the olive oil, garlic and cherry tomatoes. Let them cook for 2 minutes.

3. Spoon the penne into the garlic and tomatoes and mix everything together. Add the pesto and mix again. It will stain the pasta a beautiful green colour. Add the Parmesan, parsley and half a ladle of pasta water and give everything one final stir.

4. Plate it up and finish with a generous amount of black pepper and a final dusting of Parmesan. Yes it really is as simple as that!

IN THE BASKET

PASTA: based on 500g bag
PARMESAN: based on 60g pack

Budget Carbonara

In terms of cost this recipe has to be a winner. Before any Italians or diehard food fanatics come for me, I have to confess that this is not a traditional carbonara. The reality is that you can't buy the original Italian ingredients of guanciale, pancetta or Pecorino Romano for under a fiver today. So I'm using bacon here; it's no less tasty in my opinion. It's still an incredibly rich, creamy and beautifully indulgent pasta dish. This recipe is simplicity at its best and it's the perfect midweek dish as it takes just 10 minutes to cook from start to finish (including prep!).

Ingredients

6 eggs
80g Grana Padano, plus extra
   to serve
1 tsp black pepper, plus extra
   to serve
400g spaghetti (from a budget
   range)
250g bacon, chopped into small
   pieces

Method

1. Start by separating the egg yolks from the whites. The easiest way is to crack each egg over a bowl, catching the yolk in half the shell, then transferring it to the other half of the shell, so the white falls into the bowl. Put the yolks into a separate bowl. Collect 5 egg yolks and add 1 whole egg to them. (You can use the remaining egg whites in the Loaded Scrambled Egg, page 21, or French Toast, page 32, recipes or to make egg-fried rice with leftover rice.)

2. Add the Grana Padano and black pepper to the yolks and mix them together. They will have a paste-like texture. Set aside for later.

3. Bring a large saucepan of salted water to the boil. Add the spaghetti and cook until tender, then drain, reserving some of the cooking water.

4. Put the bacon pieces into a cold frying pan and heat it gradually (it's important to start with a cold pan as it will help to melt the bacon fat). When the bacon pieces are crisp, add the cooked spaghetti to the pan along with 2 ladles of pasta water and mix everything together.

5. Turn off the heat under the pan (so you don't scramble the yolks). Add the yolk and Grana Padano mixture and toss with the spaghetti for 2 minutes. It will start to form a creamy sauce.

6. Serve, dusting each dish with extra Grana Padano and a few cracks of black pepper.

IN THE BASKET

GRANA PADANO: based on 100g pack

SPAGHETTI: based on 500g pack

Cheesy Chorizo Fusilli

Welcome to flavour town! This recipe is always a winner in my house and the meal ends with empty plates and full stomachs! There's something about the chorizo and pasta combination that really hits the spot – it's absolutely beautiful. And combined with two balls of mozzarella this creates top tier cheese pulls.

Ingredients

300g fusilli
38 thin slices chorizo, chopped
1 red onion, finely sliced
1 red chilli, finely sliced (deseeded for a milder flavour)
5 garlic cloves, finely chopped
400g tin chopped tomatoes
2 x 125g balls mozzarella
20g (a handful) fresh parsley, finely chopped, plus extra to serve

Method

1. Bring a large saucepan of salted water to the boil. Add the pasta and cook until tender, then drain.
2. Put another pan on a medium heat and add the chorizo, onion and chilli and cook for 3–4 minutes. Add the garlic and cook for a further 2 minutes.
3. Add the tomatoes, break them up with the back of a spoon and let the sauce bubble away for another minute.
4. Spoon the pasta into the tomato and chorizo sauce and mix well. Break the balls of mozzarella into chunks and add them to the pan. Give everything a good stir and you'll see the mozzarella begin to melt and create some amazing cheese pulls.
5. Stir through the parsley and serve each portion with an extra sprinkling of it.

IN THE BASKET

PASTA: based on 500g bag

Spag Bol

It's always going to be ambitious to make a traditional ragu for under a fiver! A bottle of red wine alone would take us well over budget. But fear not, this recipe will tell you how to make a bunch of cheap ingredients into an incredible spag bol. There's no shame in using a jarred sauce, but nothing beats a homemade sauce – it's cheap, comforting, flavoursome and so easy to do. This is a family favourite and you're going to love it.

Ingredients

1 tbsp olive oil
1 onion, finely chopped
1 carrot, finely chopped
1 celery stick, finely chopped
4 garlic cloves, finely chopped
500g minced beef
1 tbsp tomato purée
400g tin chopped tomatoes
400ml beef stock (made from
   a stock cube)
400g spaghetti
salt and pepper

Method

1. Put a lidded frying pan on a medium heat and add the olive oil, onion, carrot and celery and cook them for 10 minutes until soft. Add the garlic and continue to cook for a further 2 minutes.
2. Add the mince and break it up in the pan as it cooks to make sure there are no big lumps. Season to taste with salt and pepper and cook until the meat is brown.
3. Stir through the tomato purée for 30 seconds and then add the tomatoes and stock and give everything one final stir.
4. Put on the lid and let the mixture simmer for at least 1 hour. The longer you cook it the better it gets. Keep your eye on it to make sure nothing sticks to the bottom of the pan, and give it a stir periodically, topping up with more stock if necessary.
5. After an hour, bring a saucepan of salted water to the boil. Add the spaghetti and cook until tender, then drain. Now you're ready to serve the spaghetti topped with the bolognese.

🗑 IN THE BASKET

TOMATO PUREE: based on
200g tube

STOCK: based on full pack
of cubes

SPAGHETTI: based on 1kg pack

Sausage and Tomato Penne

Every time I eat this I wonder why something so simple and cheap is so tasty. Chunks of sausage meat in a rich tomato sauce mixed through pasta make an easy midweek meal that you can chuck together after work. This might not be a traditional pasta dish and there may be some Italians out there cursing me for it, but I promise that you're going to absolutely love it.

Ingredients

8 Cumberland sausages
1 tsp olive oil, or oil spray
2 onions (from a budget range), chopped
3 garlic cloves, chopped
400g tin chopped tomatoes
400g penne
1 heaped tbsp cream cheese
10 basil leaves, plus extra to serve, finely chopped (optional)
salt and pepper

Method

1. First, skin the sausages. Take a sharp knife and score a line down the length of each sausage. The skin should peel away with ease.

2. Put a large pan (big enough to hold the sauce and the pasta) on a high heat until it's screaming hot, add a little oil and then crumble in the sausage meat. Use the back or side of a wooden spoon to break the sausage meat into smaller chunks in the pan. You want it to go a nice brown colour.

3. As soon as the meat begins to brown, add the onions and cook for 2 minutes, stirring continuously. Add the garlic and continue to cook for another 1 minute.

4. Add the tomatoes and break them up with the back of the spoon. Half fill the empty tin with water and tip that into the pan as well. Add salt and pepper to taste and simmer for 10 minutes. Keep your eye on the sauce and stir from time to time to ensure that nothing is sticking.

5. While the sauce is simmering, put the pasta on to boil in a separate pan of salted boiling water.

6. After 10 minutes, add the basil leaves to the sauce, if using, and stir them through. Add the cream cheese and give it another stir.

7. Drain the pasta and spoon it into the sausage and tomato sauce. Mix everything together thoroughly. You are now ready to serve with a scattering of some smaller basil leaves over the top.

🗑 IN THE BASKET

PASTA: based on 500g bag
CREAM CHEESE: based on 200g tub

Bacon, Mushroom, Leek and Tarragon Pasta

This recipe is a great example of just how far a fiver can stretch – it has so much flavour and is about as indulgent as it gets. It is really simple and you can throw it together in 15 minutes from start to finish (including prep). Chop all the fresh ingredients before you start so you have everything at your fingertips.

Ingredients

1 tbsp olive oil
8 bacon slices, chopped
300g mushrooms, chopped
400g spaghetti
1 leek, finely chopped
5–6 garlic cloves, finely chopped
200ml chicken stock (made from
   a stock cube)
200g cream cheese
3 tbsp tarragon leaves, finely
   chopped
salt and pepper

Method

1. Bring a large saucepan of salted water to the boil. Add the spaghetti and cook until al dente.

2. Meanwhile, put another pan on a medium heat and add the oil and bacon and cook for 2–3 minutes. As soon as the bacon starts to crisp, add the mushrooms and cook for a further 2 minutes.

3. Add the leek and garlic to the bacon and mushrooms and cook for a further minute. Pour in the stock and simmer for 3–4 minutes until it reduces slightly.

4. Stir through the cream cheese and add salt and pepper to taste.

5. As soon as the spaghetti is al dente, drain it and transfer it into the creamy sauce. Mix everything well and let it bubble away for 1 minute to finish off the pasta.

6. Add most of the tarragon and give everything one final mix before serving with a final sprinkling of tarragon leaves and black pepper.

IN THE BASKET

SPAGHETTI: based on 1kg pack

STOCK: based on full pack of cubes

Tomato and Basil Gnocchi

I don't know if you class gnocchi as pasta, but I'm going to because it's my kitchen and my rules. This is a fantastic example of how to turn some extremely cheap and humble ingredients into something quite elegant – an almost restaurant-quality dish. You can buy prepacked gnocchi, but you save money by making your own from scratch. You can make a lot of gnocchi from just a few potatoes and they can be frozen and kept for a couple of months to use when you need them. There's a bit of work in shaping the gnocchi but they're definitely worth it! And don't get me started on the tomato and basil sauce; it's so simple but it slaps you silly with flavour and pairs beautifully with the fresh gnocchi. This quantity of potatoes will make enough gnocchi to freeze some for later.

VEGETARIAN

Ingredients

1kg potatoes, peeled and cut into
  2cm chunks
1 tbsp olive oil
½ onion, finely chopped
3 garlic cloves, finely chopped
½ red chilli, finely chopped
  (deseeded for a milder flavour)
2 x 400g tins chopped tomatoes
10 basil leaves, plus extra to serve
300g plain flour
20g Parmesan
salt and pepper

Method

1. Put the potatoes in a pan, cover them with salted water and gradually bring them to the boil. Let them simmer until completely soft.

2. Put another pan on a medium heat and add the oil and the onion. Let the onion soften for 3–4 minutes. Add the garlic and chilli and continue to cook for 2 minutes. Keep everything moving around the pan to prevent it burning and sticking.

3. Add the tomatoes and then half fill one tin with water and pour that in too. Add the basil leaves and salt and pepper, give the sauce a stir, lower the heat to low and let it bubble away for 30 minutes. Check on it every 5 minutes and stir to ensure that nothing sticks.

4. The potatoes should be nice and soft now, so drain them and mash them as well as you can. Try to ensure that there are no big lumps. Season with salt to taste.

5. Tip the mashed potato on to a large board and combine it with the flour. Bring them together and knead the mixture for about a minute. It will start to resemble a dough. Divide the dough into 6 equal pieces and roll each piece into a long sausage shape. They should be be about the circumference of a £1 coin.

🛒 IN THE BASKET

FLOUR: based on 500g bag
PARMESAN: based on 60g pack

Recipe continues over the page

6. Cut the dough into 2cm long pieces. They don't need to be perfect but you can make them look more appealing by gently rolling the pieces over the back of a fork to give them a little pattern. This can take time, but you can crack open a beer or have a glass of wine and enjoy the process!

7. When you have shaped all the gnocchi; blend the tomato and basil sauce to a consistency you like (I blend mine thoroughly as my kids are fussy and don't like chunks in it). Put the sauce over a low heat to keep warm.

8. Fill a pan with water and put it on a high heat until it comes to the boil. Add a handful of gnocchi at a time and let them boil for about 1 minute. You need to cook 120g of gnocchi per person (you can freeze the rest). When the gnocchi start to float, they are ready to serve.

9. Now put another pan on a medium heat and add a ladle of tomato and basil sauce for each portion along with half a ladle of the gnocchi cooking water. Add some cooked gnocchi and toss them in the sauce until nicely combined.

10. Serve the gnocchi with a dusting of Parmesan, a crack of black pepper and a few basil leaves.

Lemon, Garlic and Chilli Spaghetti

If you only have half a brain cell and you're a terrible cook, don't worry, I've got you covered. This very simple pasta dish can be thrown together in pretty much the time it takes the spaghetti to boil and has flavours that will slap you silly (in a good way of course!).

VEGETARIAN

Ingredients

400g spaghetti

1 tbsp olive oil

8 garlic cloves, chopped

1 tsp chilli flakes

zest of 2 lemons plus the juice of 1 lemon

40g grated Parmesan, plus extra to serve

handful of fresh parsley, finely chopped, to serve

salt and pepper

Method

1. Bring a large saucepan of salted water to the boil. Add the spaghetti and cook until tender.

2. While the spaghetti is cooking put another pan on a low heat and add the oil, garlic and chilli flakes and cook for 2–3 minutes. Keep the heat low so the garlic doesn't burn.

3. By this point the spaghetti should be al dente and ready to be finished with the garlic and chilli, so transfer it into the pan and add a ladle of the pasta water. If you like it a little more liquid add more water.

4. Add the lemon zest, lemon juice, Parmesan and a teaspoon of black pepper. Toss the spaghetti in the pan for a another minute so everything is nicely combined. Add most of the parsley and give it a final toss for 20–30 seconds.

5. You're now ready to serve with a final dusting of Parmesan, black pepper and the rest of the parsley.

IN THE BASKET

SPAGHETTI: based on 1kg pack

CHILLI FLAKES: based on full jar

PARMESAN: based on 60g pack

One Pan

Fajita Rice Bowl

This is a one-pan meal fit for a king! It has so many different flavours and textures that they'll create a party in your mouth. You'll be surprised how much food you can buy for under a fiver and how effortless it is to create some serious flavour. This is perfect for a midweek dinner after work. You can also use this technique to cook the perfect rice without a rice cooker. Rice has always been tricky to get right; it's easy to let it stick to the bottom of the pan or to let it go soggy and sticky – or it's simply undercooked. Follow these simple steps and it will be spot on every time.

VEGAN

Ingredients

1 tbsp vegetable or olive oil

1 red onion, roughly chopped

1 yellow or orange pepper, roughly chopped

1 red chilli, roughly chopped, plus slices to serve (deseeded for a milder flavour)

4 garlic cloves, finely chopped

198g tin sweetcorn, drained

400g tin plum tomatoes

300g white rice, washed until the water runs clear

30g fajita seasoning

juice of ½ lime, plus lime wedges to serve

15g fresh coriander, finely chopped, plus extra to serve

1 avocado, sliced, to serve

salt and pepper

Method

1. Put a pan on a medium heat and add the oil, the onion, pepper and chilli. Let them cook for 2–3 minutes. Add the garlic and the sweetcorn and cook for a further 1 minute.

2. Add the tomatoes, break them up with the back of a wooden spoon or spatula and mix well.

3. Add the rice and the fajita seasoning and continue to stir for another minute.

4. Add 550ml boiling water, lower the heat under the pan, put on the lid and let everything bubble away for 10 minutes.

5. After 10 minutes, turn off the heat, remove the lid and cover the top of the pan with foil or a tea towel to trap the steam. Replace the lid over the foil or tea towel and let the rice steam for 15 minutes. Resist the temptation to peek inside.

6. After 15 minutes the rice will be beautifully cooked and fluffy. Stir through the coriander and squeeze in the lime juice.

7. Serve this in wide bowls and top with some sliced avocado, a few thin chilli slices, a sprinkling of coriander and a lime wedge.

IN THE BASKET

RICE: based on 1kg bag

FAJITA SEASONING: based on full jar

Tandoori Chicken Traybake

This recipe lets you switch off your brain. Chop some fresh ingredients, put them in a baking dish and put it in the oven. It really is that simple. It's probably the ultimate midweek dinner: you arrive home and within a few minutes you've got dinner cooking in the oven while you get on with other stuff such as cutting the grass or hoovering. Although it's so simple, it's definitely not lacking in flavour.

Ingredients

1kg chicken legs

3 potatoes, chopped into 2cm chunks

2 red onions, chopped into 2cm chunks

2 carrots, chopped into batons

6 garlic cloves, finely chopped

thumb-sized piece of ginger, finely chopped

2 tbsp olive oil

4 tbsp tandoori curry powder

handful of fresh coriander, finely chopped

salt and pepper

Method

1. Preheat the oven to 180°C/160°C fan/gas mark 4. Score the chicken legs to the bone.

2. Put the chicken and all the chopped vegetables into a large baking dish. Cover them in the oil and add a generous amount of salt and pepper and the tandoori curry powder. Use your hands to ensure that all the meat and veggies are coated in the seasoning. Take some time to rub it into the meat cuts too. You are aiming to add as much flavour as possible.

3. Put the chicken legs on top of the vegetables. This will help them to turn a nice golden colour in the oven. Bake in the oven for 25 minutes.

4. Take out the baking dish and turn the chicken legs over, then cook for a further 25 minutes.

5. Take the dish out of the oven and scatter over a handful of fresh coriander to serve.

IN THE BASKET

CURRY POWDER: based on full jar

One Pot Chicken and Rice

If you only own a single pan, this is the recipe for you. With hardly any effort you can make a properly tasty, healthy and filling meal. It has tons of flavour and can be made in as little as 30 minutes, including prep.

Ingredients

1kg chicken drumsticks, meat removed and bones discarded
4 tbsp chicken seasoning
1 tsp vegetable or oil
1 red onion, sliced
1 green pepper, diced
6 garlic cloves, finely chopped
400g tin chopped tomatoes
230g white rice (from budget range), washed until the water runs clear
400ml chicken stock (made from a stock cube)
salt and pepper

Method

1. Cover the meat in 3 tablespoons of the seasoning (I tend to be generous with the seasoning but use as much or as little as you like). Massage the seasoning into the meat and ensure that each piece of chicken is nicely coated.

2. Put a pan on a high heat, add a drop of oil and put the chicken pieces into the pan. Don't moving the chicken much in the pan; you're aiming for a golden-brown colour on the meat. (The chicken doesn't need to be cooked through at this point as it will be finished later.)

3. Add the onion, pepper and garlic and continue to cook for 2 minutes. Stir through the tomatoes and mix well. Add another tablespoon of seasoning and salt and pepper to taste.

4. Add the rice along with the chicken pieces and the stock, give everything another stir and put on the lid. It will take 15–20 minutes for the rice to soak up all the stock. Keep a close eye on it and give it a stir every few minutes to ensure that nothing sticks to the bottom of the pan. The texture and consistency you are aiming for is similar to a risotto.

5. When the rice is soft, it is ready to serve.

IN THE BASKET

CHICKEN SEASONING: based on full jar

RICE: based on 1kg bag

STOCK: based on full pack of cubes

Vegetable Curry

I'm always getting requests to make vegetarian meals so I thought I'd oblige. But you won't miss meat with this curry. It could almost convert me into being vegetarian (but not quite: I love fried chicken too much). As far as bang for your buck is concerned this is a winner and tastes fantastic. You can mix and match your vegetables; I use potatoes, peas and carrots but you could choose cauliflower, baby corn, broccoli, parsnips, sugar snaps or even courgettes.

VEGAN

Ingredients

2 tbsp vegetable oil

2 onions, finely chopped

2 red chillies – 1 finely chopped and 1 left whole (deseeded for a milder flavour)

6 garlic cloves, finely chopped

thumb-sized piece of ginger, finely chopped

3 tsbp curry powder

400g tin chopped tomatoes

30g fresh coriander, chopped

2 baking potatoes, chopped into 2cm chunks

2 large carrots, chopped into 2cm chunks

100g frozen peas

50g spinach

300g white rice, washed until the water runs clear, to serve

salt and pepper

IN THE BASKET

CURRY POWDER: based on full jar

PEAS: based on 800g bag

RICE: based on 1kg bag

Method

1. Put a large pan or Dutch oven on a medium heat and add the oil and onions, along with a pinch of salt, and soften them. You need to be patient with the onions; they will take at least 15 minutes to cook and brown.

2. Add the chopped chilli, garlic and ginger and continue to cook for a further 2 minutes, stirring continuously. Add the curry powder and stir for a further 30 seconds, pouring in a drop of water to stop the spices burning and sticking to the bottom of the pan.

3. Add the tomatoes with the coriander leaves and stalks (saving some of the leaves to serve later). Give it all a stir, then add the potatoes and carrots and 500ml water along with the whole chilli. Give everything another stir, put the lid on the pan and let it bubble away on a low heat for 20 minutes or until the potatoes start going soft.

4. Add the frozen peas along with the spinach and mix them through for a further 2 minutes.

5. While the curry is simmering put the rice into a pan, add 600ml boiling water and let it simmer on the lowest heat for 10 minutes. After 10 minutes, turn off the heat and cover the pot in foil to trap the residual heat. Allow it to steam for a further 15 minutes (do not be tempted to take the foil off or it will not cook properly).

6. Taste the curry and add more salt if necessary. Scatter over the remaining coriander leaves and serve with the rice.

Cowboy Stew

To experience this recipe fully I recommend making it when you go camping. There's something therapeutic about cooking a one-pan meal over an open fire (or even on a stove outside). Simply chuck the ingredients into a pan and let them bubble away to comforting perfection. The end result may not be beautiful, but it's hearty, rustic, wholesome family grub that brings a smile to your face.

Ingredients

200g bacon, chopped into pieces
8 pork sausages
1 onion, finely chopped
1 red chilli, finely chopped
    (deseeded for a milder flavour)
2 baking potatoes, cut into 2cm
    chunks
2 x 400g tins baked beans
400g tin chopped tomatoes
160g tin sweetcorn, drained
salt and pepper

Method

1. Put a large pan or casserole on a medium heat. Add the bacon and cook it until it's beautifully crisp; then take it out and set it aside for later.

2. Add the sausages and brown them all over in the bacon fat. It doesn't matter if they are not cooked through at this stage, you are just colouring them and will finish cooking them later. When they are brown all over, take them out of the pan and set them aside with the bacon.

3. Add the onion and chilli and soften for 3–4 minutes. Then add the potatoes along with the beans, tomatoes and sweetcorn and mix everything together. Fill one of the tins with water and add that to the pan too. Give it a stir, put the lid on and simmer for 15 minutes.

4. Take off the lid, return the bacon and sausages to the pan and mix again to ensure that nothing is sticking to the bottom of the pan. Let it bubble away with the lid off for a further 15 minutes (this will help to thicken it). When the potatoes have completely softened, it's ready to serve.

Honey Mustard Chicken Traybake

This is a really simple recipe and balances the sweetness of the honey against the sharpness of the mustard – when they've coated the chicken and veggies it makes them amazingly tasty! Simply chop up everything, drizzle over the sauce, chuck it in a baking dish and let the oven do the rest of the work.

Ingredients

600g carrots (from a budget range), cut into 2cm pieces
4 baking potatoes, cut into 2cm pieces
1 red onion, roughly chopped
1kg chicken drumsticks
200g honey
100g wholegrain or Dijon mustard
220g green beans
salt and pepper

Method

1. Preheat the oven to 180°C/160°C fan/gas mark 4. Place all the veggies in a large baking dish (mine is 30 x 20cm).
2. Score the drumsticks to the bone and place them on top of the veggies. Season everything generously with salt and pepper.
3. Combine the honey and mustard in a bowl and mix them together well. Drizzle the honey mustard over the drumsticks and veggies, ensuring that everything is coated as evenly as possible. Bake in the oven for 30 minutes.
4. Take out the dish and turn the drumsticks over. Return the dish to the oven and continue to cook for a further 20 minutes. You're aiming for beautifully golden crispy skin.
5. After 20 minutes add the green beans and continue to cook for a final 10 minutes.
6. Take the dish out of the oven and baste the chicken in the juices in the bottom of the baking tray, then serve.

IN THE BASKET

HONEY: based on 340g jar
MUSTARD: based on 200g jar

Spinach and Red Lentil Dahl

One for you vegans out there! I could be a vegan if it meant eating this every day for the rest of my life! It's really simple to put together and slaps on flavour. I usually pair this dish with naan bread, but you can swap that for rice or chapatis. It's up to you!

VEGAN

Ingredients

1 tbsp vegetable oil

1 onion, finely chopped

4 garlic cloves, finely chopped

thumb-sized piece of ginger, finely chopped

3 tbsp medium curry powder

400g tin plum tomatoes

300g red lentils, washed in cold water

100g spinach

naan bread or rice

salt and pepper

Method

1. Put a pan on a medium heat, add the oil and onion and soften for 3–4 minutes. Add the garlic and ginger and cook for a further minute. Add the curry powder and mix well for 30 seconds. Pour in a splash of water to prevent the curry powder sticking and burning on the bottom of the pan.

2. Add the tomatoes, breaking them up with a spoon or spatula, and mix well. Tip in the lentils and stir through for 1 minute. Pour in 1 litre of boiling water, put the lid on the pan and let it simmer on a medium heat for 15 minutes (or until the lentils have softened).

3. Season generously with salt and black pepper. Add the spinach and stir through for 2 minutes until it's completely wilted.

4. Serve with naan bread or rice of your choice.

🗑 IN THE BASKET

CURRY POWDER: based on full jar

RED LENTILS: based on 500g bag

Mushroom and Broccoli Stir Fry

This very basic stir fry will get you out of trouble when you're skint and struggling to make it to the end of the month. It has all sorts of flavours – garlicky, spicy, salty – and a fantastic crunch from the broccoli! It's really simple and you're going to love it. If you can increase your budget you could use chicken instead of the mushrooms. Always start by prepping and chopping up the fresh ingredients; you want to have everything at your fingertips as it cooks incredibly fast.

VEGAN

Ingredients

1 tbsp vegetable oil
300g mushrooms, roughly chopped
1 head broccoli, broken into florets
2 red chillies, finely sliced
   (deseeded for a milder flavour)
6 garlic cloves, finely chopped
500g noodles
100ml soy sauce
salt and pepper

Method

1. Put a wok or deep pan on a high heat until it's screaming hot and add the oil and the mushrooms. Try not to move them around much; you want them to go a nice brown colour.

2. When the mushrooms are coloured, add the broccoli, 1 of the chillies and the garlic. Toss for 2 minutes.

3. As soon as the broccoli begins to soften, add the noodles and the soy sauce. Give everything another mix and cook for a further 2 minutes.

4. Plate up and serve with the second sliced chilli.

IN THE BASKET

SOY SAUCE: based on
150ml bottle

Chilli Con Carne

This is a versatile dish that you can pair with many different things; have it with rice, smother it over fries, put it on a hot dog, pour it over a jacket spud or just dip in some tortilla chips. It can be frozen as well, so it's great for saving time on meal prep! I use store-bought chilli con carne seasoning, but if you have a lot of spices in your cupboard (cumin, chilli powder, paprika, cumin seeds) then you're on to a winner. This is so simple and it absolutely slaps with flavour.

Ingredients

1 tsp vegetable or olive oil
1 onion, finely chopped
4 garlic cloves, finely chopped
2 green chillies, finely chopped,
    plus 1 to serve
500g minced beef
41g packet of chilli con carne
    seasoning
400g tin chopped tomatoes
130g tin kidney beans, drained
300ml beef stock (made with a
    stock cube)
salt and pepper

Method

1. Put a pan on a medium heat and add the oil and the onion and soften for 3–4 minutes. Add the garlic and chillies and continue to cook for a further 2 minutes. If you're not keen on a lot of spice just use 1 chilli and remove the seeds.

2. Add the mince and break it up with the back of a spoon, ensuring that there's no big lumps. Cook the meat until it's nice and brown. Be generous with the salt and pepper and then add the chilli con carne seasoning. Mix well.

3. Add the tomatoes and kidney beans and stir. Then pour in the beef stock and simmer for 30 minutes. The simmering is very important (it's like a fine wine that gets better with age).

4. Serve with sliced chilli.

BBQ Seasoned Chicken and Veg Traybake

I live in an incredibly busy household; we have 3 kids and we live life at a hundred miles an hour. It's rare that I find time on a weekday to cook up a storm. By the time I've got in from work I don't have the energy to do anything fancy. That's where this traybake comes in. It's quite literally as simple as putting everything in a baking dish and whacking it in the oven for 50 minutes. I reckon even my four-year-old daughter could do it!

Ingredients

3 baking potatoes, cut into 2–3cm chunks

1 courgette, cut into 2–3cm chunks

1 red pepper, cut into 2–3cm chunks

1 red onion, cut into 2–3cm chunks

3 tomatoes, cut into 2–3cm chunks

1 garlic bulb, chopped

1kg chicken drumsticks

5 tbsp olive oil

5 tbsp BBQ seasoning

salt and pepper

Method

1. Preheat the oven to 180°C/160°C fan/gas mark 4.
2. Put the chopped vegetables into a baking dish along with the drumsticks. Cover in the oil, BBQ seasoning and a generous quantity of salt and black pepper. Use your hands to rub the seasoning into the meat and veggies until they are all evenly coated.
3. Arrange the dish so the drumsticks sit on the top of the veggies. This will allow them to go a nice brown colour in the oven as they cook, while the vegetables soak up the chicken juices.
4. Bake in the oven for 50 minutes, then serve.

IN THE BASKET

BBQ SEASONING: based on full jar

Chicken Curry

A recipe for a fiver has never looked so good. This is a proper classic that you will make time and time again. I make this with chicken drumsticks because there's more flavour in meat on the bone – the fact that it's cheaper is a bonus! I love it when I see meat falling off the bone because it's just so tender! If you're fussy about meat on the bone you can increase your budget and use boneless thighs or even breasts. This basic but incredibly flavoursome and versatile recipe can be served with rice, naan, on a jacket spud or even smothered over some chunky chips!

Ingredients

2 tbsp vegetable oil

2 onions, finely chopped

6 garlic cloves, finely chopped

thumb-sized piece of ginger, finely chopped

2 red chillies, 1 finely chopped (deseeded for a milder flavour), 1 whole

3 tbsp curry powder

400g tin chopped tomatoes

30g fresh coriander, chopped

1kg chicken drumsticks

300g white rice (from budget range), washed until the water runs clear, to serve

salt and pepper

Method

1. Start by putting a large pan on a medium heat and adding the oil, the onion and a teaspoon of salt, then let the onions soften for at least 15 minutes. Be patient with them and take them to the edge of burning. You want them to be nice and caramelised. Give them a stir every now and again to ensure they are not sticking to the pan or burning.

2. Add the garlic, ginger and the finely-chopped chilli and cook for 2 more minutes. Add the curry powder and give it a stir. Now add a drop of water to prevent the spices burning and give everything another stir.

3. Add the tomatoes and half the coriander, including all the stalks (there's so much flavour in the stalks).

4. Add the drumsticks and cover everything with 500ml water. Now add the whole chilli. Bring the liquid to a simmer, put on the lid and let it bubble away for 30 minutes. Check on it every now and again to make sure nothing sticks to the bottom of the pan.

5. While the curry is simmering start the rice to serve with it. Put it in a pan with 600ml boiling water and simmer on the lowest heat for 10 minutes. Turn off the heat completely and cover the pan with foil to trap the residual heat. Allow it to steam for a further 15 minutes. Do not take off the foil or it will not cook properly.

6. After 30 minutes take the lid off the curry pan; the meat should be tender and falling off the bone. Let it bubble away for a further 5–10 minutes with the lid off until the sauce has thickened.

7. Serve the curry on rice, topped with the rest of the coriander leaves.

IN THE BASKET

CURRY POWDER: based on full jar

RICE: based on 1kg bag

Mushroom Risotto

This is probably the simplest risotto recipe you're ever going to lay your eyes on – all you have to do is buy six ingredients. This recipe delivers on flavour every time. I'm skipping the white wine because booze is expensive, but if you've got it lying around in the fridge add a couple of glugs before you start adding the stock. The key to a good risotto is patience; it can take 20 to 25 minutes for the rice to absorb all the stock. Don't rush it; take your time and enjoy the cooking process.

Ingredients

1 tbsp olive oil
1 onion, finely diced
3 garlic cloves, finely chopped
300g mushrooms, roughly chopped
350g risotto rice
1200ml hot chicken stock (made from a stock cube)
30g grated Parmesan, plus extra to serve
salt and pepper
handful of fresh parsley, finely chopped, to serve (optional)

Method

1. Put a pan on a medium heat and add the oil, onion and some salt and pepper. Cook for 3–4 minutes until the onion has softened. Add the garlic and cook for 1 minute, then the mushrooms and cook for 2–3 minutes. Add the rice and mix it with the mushrooms for 1 minute.

2. Pour the stock into a saucepan on a low heat. Add the stock, a ladle at a time, for the next 20–25 minutes. You need to stir the rice continuously and every time it absorbs a ladleful of stock, add another one. Repeat until the rice is soft and plump – you're aiming for a creamy texture.

3. Add the grated Parmesan and mix well.

4. Plate up the risotto and sprinkle another dusting of Parmesan on top with some parsley, if using.

IN THE BASKET

RISOTTO RICE: based on 500g bag

STOCK: based on full pack of cubes

PARMESAN: based on 60g pack

Chorizo Paella

Somebody once asked me to make a 'poverty spec' paella and this I what I came up with – and what a banger of a one-pan meal this is! It has so much in it and it's hard to believe that it costs less than a fiver. It's very simple and you're going to love it. I use a packet of paella seasoning to keep costs down, but if you have traditional paella seasoning in your cupboards (paprika, cumin, turmeric, cayenne, onion powder, garlic powder, and so on) then use those instead.

Ingredients

1 tbsp vegetable or olive oil
180g chorizo, cut into small pieces
1 red onion, diced
1 yellow or orange pepper, diced
6 garlic cloves, finely chopped
300g white rice (from budget range), washed, soaked in cold water and drained
30g paella seasoning
630ml chicken stock (made from a stock cube)
100g frozen peas
squeeze of lemon juice, plus slices to serve
salt and pepper

Method

1. Put a pan on a medium heat, add the oil and chorizo and cook for 1 minute, stirring continuously. Add the onion and pepper and continue to cook for 2 minutes, stirring. Add the garlic and cook for a further minute.

2. Add the rice with the paella seasoning and mix well for 2 minutes to allow the uncooked rice to take on the flavours of the pan.

3. Add the chicken stock, put on the lid, turn the heat as low as possible and let everything bubble away for 10 minutes. Avoid taking the lid off the pan; you want the heat to be contained.

4. After 10 minutes add the frozen peas and give everything a mix to make sure nothing is sticking to the bottom. Cover the pan in foil to ensure no steam escapes and put the lid back on. Turn the heat off and leave everything to steam for 15 minutes. Do not peek under the foil.

5. After 15 minutes take off the foil and run a fork through the rice; it should be nice and fluffy and not at all sticky.

6. Add a squeeze of lemon juice with salt and pepper to taste. Serve with slices of lemon.

🧺 IN THE BASKET

RICE: based on 1kg bag

PAELLA SEASONING: based on full jar

STOCK: based on full pack of cubes

PEAS: based on 850g bag

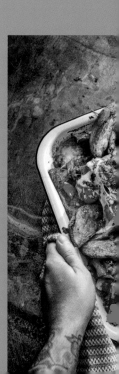

Sharing Foods

Tandoori-style Chicken Wings

These might be the easiest to make (as well as the cheapest) chicken wings you'll ever eat – oven baked to perfection and so tender that the meat almost falls off the bone. With this type of dish you might tell yourself that you'll just eat a couple of wings, but then you'll end up eating 15 of them. They're very moreish and once you start eating them you won't be able to stop!

Ingredients

1kg chicken wings, trimmed
4 tbsp natural yoghurt
6 garlic cloves, finely chopped
thumb-sized piece of ginger, finely
   chopped
juice of 1 lemon
2 tbsp tandoori curry powder
handful of fresh coriander, finely
   chopped, to serve
salt and pepper

Method

1. Put the wings in a bowl with the yoghurt, garlic, ginger, lemon juice, tandoori curry powder and some salt and pepper. Use your hands to massage the seasoning into the wings, ensuring that every wing has some seasoning.

2. Cover the bowl in cling film and put it in the fridge to marinate for at least 2 hours, or preferably overnight.

3. Preheat the oven to 180°C /160°C fan/gas mark 4. Put the wings on a baking tray and bake them in the oven for 20 minutes. Turn the wings and then put them back into the oven for a further 20 minutes.

4. They should now be very tender with the meat almost ready to fall off the bone! Add some more salt as a finishing touch and serve with the coriander.

IN THE BASKET

YOGHURT: based in 500g tub

CURRY POWDER: based on
full jar

Crispy Salt and Pepper Chicken Wings

Crispy, salty, spicy, juicy – this is about as indulgent as food gets! Believe it or not you can make Chinese takeaway style salt and pepper wings in the comfort of your own home at a fraction of the cost. I've taken these up a level and coated them in a Chinese five-spice batter so they are extra crispy! You will love them and I recommend you give them a go. You will need a deep-fat fryer, or a saucepan and a cooking thermometer, as well as oil for deep frying, but the oil can be cooled and stored so you can use it five or six times, making it pretty cost-effective. If you're not a fan of meat on the bone you can use the same method with chunks of boneless thigh or breast meat instead of wings.

Ingredients

500g plain flour
2 tsp Chinese five spice
1kg chicken wings, trimmed
1 litre vegetable oil, for deep frying,
    plus 1 tbsp to fry vegetables
1 onion, roughly chopped
1 yellow or orange pepper, roughly
    chopped
1 red chilli, finely chopped, plus
    slices to serve (deseeded for a
    milder flavour)
1 garlic bulb, cloves finely chopped
4 spring onions, chopped
salt and pepper

Method

1. Divide the flour equally between two bowls and add 1 teaspoon of Chinese five spice to each bowl along with salt and pepper to taste.

2. Gradually add 350ml water to one of the bowls, mixing all the time to turn the flour into a batter.

3. Now coat the wings; put one wing at a time into the seasoned flour, then dunk it in the batter and double dip it back into the seasoned flour. Repeat this with all the wings until they are generously coated.

4. Heat the oil in a deep-fat fryer to 180°C. Do not remove the basket but carefully put the wings into the hot oil inside it and deep fry the wings for 8–10 minutes until they are beautifully golden. (This prevents the wings from sticking to the bottom of the basket.) If you don't have a deep-fat fryer, heat 1 litre oil (or enough oil to cover the wings) in a large saucepan to 180°C. Put the wings carefully into the hot oil one at a time, on the side of the saucepan furthest from you (to avoid splashes), and cook them for 8–10 minutes until they are golden brown. Don't overcrowd the pan or the wings will stick together.

5. When the wings are cooked, carefully remove them and lay them on kitchen paper to drain.

6. Put a frying pan on a high heat until it is screaming hot (to the point where it is smoking), add a tablespoon of oil and then the onion, pepper and chilli. Toss them for 2 minutes until they begin to soften. Add the garlic and cook for a further 1 minute.

🗑 **IN THE BASKET**

CHINESE 5-SPICE: based on full jar

7. Add the crispy wings to the pan and toss them for 30 seconds.
8. Salt generously and finish with the spring onions. Give everything a final toss to ensure that is all mixed well. Serve with slices of chilli.

Bloomer Loaf Pizzas

This is a great and simple recipe that I love making with my kids. It's so versatile and you can adapt it to your own preferences! My kids tend to be quite fussy and opt for a classic margherita style pizza, but I like to load up with pepperoni, jalapeños, red onion and peppers. You do whatever you fancy. Go wild with it – you only live once.

ⁱⁱⁱⁱ/ⁱ

Ingredients

800g large unsliced bloomer loaf
200g tomato purée
2 x 125g mozzarella balls
70g sliced pepperoni
1 green pepper, finely sliced
½ red onion, finely sliced
pickled jalapeños, to taste
salt and pepper

Method

1. Preheat the oven to 190°C /170°C fan/gas mark 5. Slice the loaf in half horizontally to make two large pizza bases.

2. Squeeze the tomato purée into a bowl and gradually mix in a little water until it's the consistency of mayonnaise or mustard. Spoon the purée on to the bread and spread it out.

3. Break up the balls of mozzarella and spread the pieces equally across the pizza bases.

4. Now add the the pepperoni, pepper, onion slices and jalapeños.

5. Put the pizza bases on a baking tray and bake them for 15 minutes or until the mozzarella starts to go golden.

6. Take the pizzas out of the oven, slice and serve.

Battered Curry Chips

This recipe is living proof that you don't need to spend a ton of money to eat something that's properly indulgent and comforting. I would say that this is the definition of a proper Wolverhampton (my home town!) chip. Absolutely gorgeous. You will need a deep-fat fryer, or a saucepan and a cooking thermometer, as well as oil for deep frying, but the oil can be cooled and stored so you can make good use of it and use it five or six times.

VEGAN

Ingredients

1.4 kg baking potatoes, cut into
   thick chips or wedges
500g plain flour
3 tbsp curry powder
1 litre vegetable oil for deep frying,
   plus 1 tbsp extra
1 onion, thinly sliced
2 red chillies, thinly sliced,
   deseeded for a milder flavour
4 garlic cloves, finely chopped
handful of fresh coriander,
   chopped
salt and pepper

Method

1. Fill a pan with water and bring it to a rolling boil, add a pinch of salt and then the chips. Parboil them for 10 minutes or until a fork pierces them easily. Drain them and let them dry for about 10 minutes.

2. Divide the flour equally between two bowls. Put a heaped tablespoon of curry powder in each bowl along with some salt and pepper to taste and give them a mix.

3. Gradually add water to one of the bowls, mixing continuously to form a batter. You will need about 400ml water. The batter should be the consistency of paint and have no lumps of flour.

4. One by one, dredge the chips first in the flour, then the batter and then back in the flour again. Repeat this until they are all coated in batter and flour – be patient; it can be a messy process. I recommend using one hand for the flour and the other for the batter, so your hands don't get too messy.

5. Heat the oil in a deep-fat fryer to 180°C, then deep-fry the chips for 5 minutes until the batter is golden brown and crisp. If you don't have a deep-fat fryer, heat 1 litre oil in a large saucepan to 180°C. Put the chips carefully into the hot oil and deep-fry them for 5 minutes until they are golden brown. Try not to overcrowd the pan or the chips will stick together. Fry them in batches if necessary.

6. When you take the chips out, season them generously with salt. They will be crisp on the outside and soft and fluffy inside.

7. To take the chips to another level, heat a frying pan on a high heat until it is screaming hot and add a drop of oil. Add the onion and chillies and cook for 2 minutes. Add the garlic and cook for a further 1 minute.

IN THE BASKET

CURRY POWDER: based on
full jar

8. Add a tablespoon of curry powder, give it a stir and then put in the battered chips. Sprinkle over another pinch of salt and give the contents of the pan a good toss until everything is well combined.

9. Finish the chips with a generous handful of coriander and they are ready to serve.

Kofta with Homemade Flatbreads

This recipe costs just £1.25 per portion (at the time of writing) and what you make will surprise you: a properly homemade kofta-style kebab in a flatbread – with some salad too. It's not difficult to make; just chuck the ingredients into a bowl, mix them together, shape them round skewers and grill them. To keep costs down I've based the seasoning on a prepacked doner kebab mix, which contains a bit of everything (onion powder, cinnamon, garlic powder, oregano, thyme, bay and so on) but as always, if you have your own seasoning in the cupboard, feel free to use that.

Ingredients

250g self-raising flour, plus extra for kneading

250g natural yoghurt, plus extra to serve

2 tbsp olive or vegetable oil, plus extra for frying

500g minced beef (20% fat)

1 onion, grated

4 garlic cloves, minced

handful of fresh mint, finely chopped, plus extra to serve

38g doner kebab seasoning mix

1 iceberg lettuce, finely shredded

1 red onion, finely diced

salt and pepper

Method

1. Mix the flour, yoghurt, 1 teaspoon salt and 1 tablespoon of the oil in a bowl until they start to form a dough. Flour a board, knead the dough for 3–4 minutes, then put it back into the bowl to rest while you make the kofta.

2. Put the mince, onion, garlic, mint, doner seasoning, salt and pepper (be quite generous) and 1 tablespoon of the oil into a large bowl. Use your hands to mix and squeeze everything together, making sure that the meat is mixed well with the flavourings.

3. If you have time, leave the mixture to marinate for a couple of hours (or even overnight) for the flavours to develop. Otherwise you can continue straight away.

4. Use skewers to help shape the meat and divide it into four equal pieces (if you dip your hands in cold water it will prevent the meat sticking to your hands). Carefully wrap a lump of the meat mixture around a skewer and mould it into a cylinder shape. Repeat with all four skewers – you should be able to make 4 koftas about 18–20cm long from this quantity.

5. Put a griddle pan on a high heat and add a tiny splash of oil (the meat is quite fatty so you won't need much). Put the koftas into the pan and very carefully remove the skewers to ensure that all the meat is in contact with the pan surface. You could also barbecue the skewers for a more authentic flavour.

6. Cook the koftas until they are seared all over; they should take 2 minutes on each side to cook through. Take care as they can be fragile and break quite easily.

7. Divide the flatbread dough into four equal pieces, flour the board and roll them to the thickness of a £1 coin). This may seem a little thin but they will rise as they cook.

8. Put a griddle pan on a high heat and grill the flatbreads for 2 minutes on each side until they have black char marks on both sides.

9. To assemble, spread a tablespoon of natural yoghurt over a flatbread and add some lettuce and red onion. Lay the kofta on top and finally sprinkle over some mint.

IN THE BASKET

FLOUR: based on 500g bag

YOGHURT: based on 500g tub

Margherita Pizzas

I love picking up the phone and ordering a Domino's – but have you seen how expensive takeaway pizzas are these days? Crazy money. If you want to eat pizza for hardly any money this is the recipe for you. I make these pizzas with my kids all the time; it's a good opportunity to keep them occupied and save a fortune in the process. You'll be able to make four 12-inch pizzas from this recipe and if you want to make them even more special you can increase your budget and add more toppings!

VEGETARIAN

Ingredients

500g plain flour, plus extra for kneading
300ml lukewarm water
7g yeast
400g tin chopped tomatoes
1 garlic clove
1 tsp dried oregano
handful of basil leaves
2 x 125g balls of mozzarella, broken into pieces
olive oil (optional), to serve
salt and pepper

Method

1. Put the flour and ½ teaspoon salt into a bowl. Mix the water and yeast in a jug. Slowly pour the yeast water into the bowl, bit by bit, mixing all the time. It will eventually form a dough.

2. Flour a board and knead the dough for 5 minutes until it has some elasticity.

3. Put the dough back in the bowl, cover it with a cold damp tea towel and leave it to rise for 1 hour. It's important to leave it for a full hour to allow the yeast to work its magic.

4. While the dough is rising put the tomatoes, garlic, oregano, 6 basil leaves and some salt and pepper into a food processor. Blitz them until they are smooth.

5. Preheat the oven to its highest setting. When the dough has doubled in size; flour the board again and divide the dough into 4 equal pieces. Roll each piece to the thickness of a £1 coin. The dough should be quite stretchy so you can shape it however you like. The pizzas don't need to be perfect; I like mine rustic and a little messy. Lightly fold in the edges of the dough by about 1cm to form a crust on each pizza and place on a pizza or baking tray.

6. Spoon the tomato sauce on to the pizzas and then top with pieces of mozzarella (add extra toppings now if you'd like some).

7. Cook the pizzas for about 5–6 minutes, or until the crusts are beautifully crisp and the mozzarella is melted and golden.

8. Serve with fresh basil leaves and a drizzle of olive oil.

IN THE BASKET

FLOUR: based on 1.5kg bag
YEAST: based on 57g pack
OREGANO: based on full jar

Crispy Garlic Parmesan Wings

I love chicken wings – they're cheap, versatile and incredibly tasty. I developed this recipe because everyone in my house was moaning that I make wings too spicy or too juicy and they make a mess. So this recipe is super mellow and even my kids eat them, so they must be good! The combination of garlic, Parmesan and chives is a thing of beauty and you won't have to dig deep into your pockets. You will need a deep-fat fryer, or a saucepan and a cooking thermometer, as well as oil for deep frying, but the oil can be cooled and stored so you can use it five or six times.

Ingredients

100g plain flour
50g grated Parmesan
1kg chicken wings, trimmed
1 litre vegetable oil for deep frying,
    plus 1 tbsp extra
6 garlic cloves, finely chopped
15g fresh chives, chopped
salt and pepper

Method

1. Put the flour, a little salt and pepper and 20g of the Parmesan into a large bowl (don't add much salt as Parmesan is quite salty). Mix until everything is combined. Add the chicken wings to the bowl and coat them in the mixture, shake off any excess flour and set them aside.

2. Heat the oil in a deep-fat fryer to 180°C. Do not remove the basket but carefully put the wings into the hot oil inside it and deep fry the wings for 10 minutes until they are golden and crispy. (This prevents the wings from sticking to the bottom of the basket.) If you don't have a deep-fat fryer, heat 1 litre oil (or enough oil to cover the wings) in a large saucepan to 180°C. Put the wings carefully into the hot oil one at a time, on the side of the saucepan furthest from you (to avoid splashes), and cook them for 10 minutes until they are golden. Don't overcrowd the pan or the wings will stick together. You could also cook them in an air fryer (timings may vary).

3. When the wings are cooked lay them on kitchen paper and season them lightly with salt.

4. Put a pan on a low heat and add 1 tablespoon of cooking oil followed by the garlic. Cook for 2 minutes until the garlic is fragrant and then add the crispy chicken wings.

5. Toss the wings in the garlic for 30 seconds, then add 20g of the Parmesan followed by half the chives. Toss again for a further 30 seconds and take off the heat.

6. Serve the wings with the remaining Parmesan and chives.

🗑 **IN THE BASKET**

FLOUR: based on 500g bag
PARMESAN: based on 60g pack

Loaded Fajita Wedges

This recipe is properly indulgent: crispy wedges soaked in a fajita-flavoured sauce, topped with mozzarella and grilled to cheese-pull perfection. It's up to you how you cook up your wedges – I've based this recipe on oven baking them. Alternatively, you can parboil them for 10 minutes and then deep fry them to finish. Or you could cook them in an air fryer. This is a great little recipe for party food on a match day or as part of a buffet. Everyone can grab a bowl and dig in.

VEGETARIAN

Ingredients

8 baking potatoes, sliced into thick wedges (about 8 per potato)

1 tbsp vegetable or olive oil, plus extra for drizzling

30g fajita seasoning, from a packet

1 onion, roughly chopped

1 yellow or orange pepper, roughly chopped

1 red chilli, roughly chopped, plus slices to serve, deseeded for a milder flavour

4 garlic cloves, finely chopped

400g tin chopped tomatoes

125g ball of mozzarella

15g fresh coriander, finely chopped, to serve

salt and pepper

Method

1. Preheat the oven to 180°C/160°C fan/gas mark 4 and place the wedges on 2 baking trays, spaced so they're not overcrowded.

2. Drizzle oil over the wedges followed by some salt and pepper and half the fajita seasoning, saving the rest for later. Bake in the oven for 45 minutes.

3. Just before the wedges are cooked, put a pan on a medium heat and pour in a tablespoon of oil. Add the onion, pepper and chilli followed by some salt and pepper. Let this cook for 3–4 minutes until it begins to soften. Add the garlic and cook for a further 1 minute.

4. Add the remaining seasoning and stir for another minute; keep everything moving so the seasoning doesn't burn on the bottom of the pan. Stir through the tomatoes and let the sauce bubble away for 2 minutes.

5. Take the wedges out of the oven. By this point they should be crispy on the outside and fluffy on the inside. Put them in a baking dish (I use a 25 x 20cm dish). Spoon over the sauce and spread it over the wedges. Break up the mozzarella ball and spread the pieces over too. Heat the grill.

6. Put the baking dish under the hot grill for 5 minutes (or until the cheese has melted and is beautifully golden). Serve with the fresh coriander and sliced chilli scattered over the top.

Vegetable Quesadillas

You don't need meat in quesadillas to make them tasty; these are properly exciting and there isn't a piece of chicken in sight! For this recipe I use store-bought fajita seasoning to save the pennies, but if you have paprika, onion powder, garlic powder, cumin, oregano and chilli powder in your cupboard then use those instead. These quesadillas are very simple and will take just 15 minutes to cook (including prep). Start by preparing all the fresh ingredients so you have everything to hand.

VEGETARIAN

Ingredients

1 tbsp vegetable or olive oil
1 red onion, thinly sliced
1 yellow or orange pepper, diced
1 courgette, diced
2 tomatoes, diced
198g tin sweetcorn, drained
3 garlic cloves, finely chopped
30g fajita seasoning
15g fresh coriander, finely chopped
4–5 corn tortillas
125g ball mozzarella
salt and pepper

Method

1. Put a pan on a medium-high heat and add the oil, onion, pepper, courgette and tomatoes. Season with salt and pepper and give everything a mix. Cook for 2–3 minutes until everything begins to soften.

2. Add the sweetcorn and garlic and cook for a further minute, then stir through the fajita seasoning and cook for a minute more.

3. Add the coriander (saving some to serve) and give it one final stir. Take the pan off the heat and set it aside. That's the filling done.

4. Put a griddle pan on a high heat until it is screaming hot, then add one of the tortillas. Break off a few chunks of the mozzarella and scatter them across the tortilla. You're aiming to fill 4–5 tortillas with the filling you've made so ensure that every tortilla has a portion of mozzarella.

5. When the cheese begins to melt, spoon roughly a quarter of the filling on to the right hand side of the tortilla. Carefully fold the left half of the tortilla over the filling to create a semicircle.

6. Cook the tortilla for 30 seconds so there are griddle marks on both sides. Repeat until you have cooked all the tortillas and used all the filling.

7. Cut the quesadillas in half and serve with the remaining coriander.

IN THE BASKET

FAJITA SEASONING: based on full jar

TORTILLAS: based on full pack

Cheesy Bacon Spuds

These are an absolute treat – is there a better combination than cheese and bacon? These spuds are so indulgent and moreish that I know for a fact that you will demolish the entire plate. They taste really creamy with a fantastic saltiness from the bits of bacon. And don't get me started on the cheese pulls from the mozzarella; gorgeous!

Ingredients

8 baking potatoes
8 bacon slices
20g chives, finely chopped
200g cream cheese
2 x 125g balls mozzarella, broken into pieces
salt and pepper

Method

1. Preheat the oven to 190°C/170°C fan/gas mark 5. Pierce the potatoes all over with a fork, rub a generous amount of salt over their skins and wrap them individually in foil. Bake them in the oven for 1½ hours.
2. When the potatoes have 20 minutes still to cook, put the bacon slices on a baking tray in the oven and cook them until crispy.
3. Take everything out of the oven and cut the bacon into small pieces. Remove the potatoes from the foil, cut them in half and spoon the flesh into a bowl. Try not to split the skins as you will need them later.
4. Add salt and pepper, the chopped bacon, chives (saving some to serve), cream cheese and half the mozzarella. Mash everything together until it's well combined.
5. Spoon the potato mixture back into the skins, break up the other ball of mozzarella and spread it evenly on top. Put the potatoes back in the oven for 10 minutes until the mozzarella is golden.
6. Serve with the remaining chives.

Lemon, Garlic and Herb Chicken Wings

If like me you love a ton of garlic in your food, this is definitely a recipe for you. It's perfect for sharing, or you could eat the whole lot yourself – whatever floats your boat. Serve these wings as a match-day snack or even just a little treat when you have the family over for a barbecue in the summer. They're simple to make and really pack a punch!

Ingredients

1kg chicken wings, trimmed

zest of 2 and juice of 3 lemons, from a budget range

2 tsp dried mixed herbs

6 garlic cloves, finely chopped

5 tbsp olive oil

20g (a handful) fresh parsley, chopped, plus extra to serve

salt and pepper

Method

1. Put the wings in a bowl and add the lemon zest and juice of 2 of the lemons, 1 teaspoon of the mixed herbs, the garlic, 1 tablespoon of the olive oil, the parsley and salt and pepper to taste. Use your hands to mix everything together and make sure that every wing has some herbs and seasoning.

2. When everything is combined, cover the bowl with cling film and put it in the fridge to marinate for at least 2 hours, or preferably overnight – the longer the better.

3. While the wings are marinating make the basting sauce. In another bowl, put 4 tablespoons of olive oil, the lemon juice and the remaining mixed herbs and mix well.

4. The ideal way to cook the wings is on an outdoor flame grill or barbecue. Make sure the barbecue grill is screaming hot before you start and flip the wings every 2 minutes until they are cooked through. Every time you flip the wings, baste them with the lemon and herb sauce. You're aiming for grill marks and some charring. Alternatively, preheat the oven to 180°C/160°C fan/gas mark 4 and bake the wings for 40 minutes, flipping them after 20 minutes.

5. Serve the wings with fresh parsley scattered over the top.

IN THE BASKET

MIXED HERBS: based on full jar

Halloumi Tacos with Tomato Salsa and Chilli Yoghurt

This recipe offers you an amazing spread for a fiver. When all all the food is laid out on the table you'll be rubbing your eyes in disbelief at the low cost. There are so many elements with many different flavours and textures – it's a party in your mouth! I've always loved varied finger food that allows everyone to eat a bit of everything.

VEGETARIAN

Ingredients

225g halloumi, cut into thin batons
2 garlic cloves, finely chopped
   (optional)
For the tortillas
250g plain flour, plus extra
   for kneading
1 tsp salt
130ml warm water
1 tbsp olive oil
For the salsa
3 tomatoes, finely chopped
½ red onion, finely chopped
½ red chilli, finely chopped
   (deseeded for a milder flavour)
2 tbsp fresh coriander, finely
   chopped, plus extra to serve
1 tsp olive oil
juice of ¼ lime
For the chilli yoghurt
300ml natural yoghurt
juice of ¼ lime
1 red chilli, finely chopped, plus
   slices to serve
salt and pepper

IN THE BASKET

FLOUR: based on 500g bag
YOGHURT: based on 500g tub

Method

1. Start by making the dough for the tortillas. Combine all the ingredients in a bowl and bring them together. Flour a board and knead the dough for 5 minutes (you can add a touch more flour if the dough is loose). Put the dough back in the bowl and let it rest for 15 minutes.

2. To prepare the salsa, put the tomatoes, onion, chilli and coriander in a bowl with some salt and pepper, the oil and lime juice. Taste it and tweak the flavours to your liking, adding more lime juice or more coriander.

3. Put all the yoghurt ingredients in a bowl and mix them together. I like to add slices of chilli on top to serve (makes it look pretty!).

4. When the dough has rested; flour the board again and divide the dough into 6 equal pieces. Roll the balls to the thickness of a £1 coin. They don't need to be perfect circles – sometimes they look better different shapes, adding a rustic look to the meal.

5. Put a griddle pan on a high heat until it is screaming hot and cook the tortillas one at a time for about 1 minute on each side. You are aiming to give them some black char marks. Repeat until all the tortillas are cooked, then set them aside with the salsa and yoghurt.

6. Cook the halloumi under a hot grill or in another hot frying pan for 1 minute on each side until it is a golden brown colour. When you turn the halloumi add the garlic, if using, and cook for a minute.

7. Everyone can grab a tortilla, smother it in the yoghurt, then a couple of spoons of salsa, top it with a few slices of halloumi, give it a squeeze of lime juice and add coriander and sliced chilli.

Crispy Buttermilk Fried Chicken

This recipe would give KFC a run for its money at a quarter of the price. When you think of comfort food, fried chicken has to be at the top of the list. Picture it now: super crispy on the outside but incredibly juicy on the inside! The great thing about this recipe is that there's hardly any messing about and you only need to buy four items. So it's simple, but definitely not lacking in flavour. I use an all-purpose smoky BBQ seasoning for this recipe, but if you have these herbs and spices in your cupboard then you're an even bigger winner: 1 teaspoon dried thyme, 1 tablespoon paprika, 3 teaspoons garlic powder, 1 teaspoon mustard powder, 1 teaspoon dried oregano, 1 tablespoon onion powder, 1 teaspoon celery salt, 1 teaspoon cayenne, 1 teaspoon ground ginger, salt and black pepper. You will need a deep-fat fryer, or a saucepan and a cooking thermometer, as well as oil for deep frying, but the oil can be cooled and stored so you can use it five or six times.

Ingredients

300ml buttermilk
10 tsp smoky BBQ seasoning
1kg chicken drumsticks
150g plain flour
1 litre vegetable oil, for deep frying
salt and pepper

IN THE BASKET

BBQ SEASONING: based on full jar

FLOUR: based on 500g bag

Method

1. Put the buttermilk, 1 teaspoon salt, 1 teaspoon pepper and 5 teaspoons of the BBQ seasoning into a large bowl. Mix well, ensuring that the seasoning and buttermilk are nicely combined.

2. Put the drumsticks in the bowl and give everything another mix. Don't be afraid to use your hands – it's easier to coat the drumsticks by hand.

3. Cover the bowl with cling film and put it in the fridge to marinate. You can leave it for as little as 2 hours, but for best results leave it overnight.

4. When you're ready to cook the drumsticks, put the flour, a teaspoon of salt, a teaspoon of pepper and the remaining BBQ seasoning into another large bowl and stir until combined.

5. Put the drumsticks into the seasoned flour one at a time and coat them evenly and generously. The buttermilk will help the flour stick to the drumsticks. Repeat until all the drumsticks are coated.

6.   Heat a deep-fat fryer to 160°C. I keep the temperature relatively
     low so you don't end up with a burnt outside and a raw inside. Do
     not remove the basket but carefully put the drumsticks into the
     hot oil inside it and deep fry them for 12–15 minutes until they are
     beautifully golden and crispy. (This prevents the drumsticks from
     sticking to the bottom of the basket.) If you don't have a deep-fat
     fryer, heat 1 litre oil (or enough oil to cover the drumsticks) in a large
     saucepan to 180°C. Put the drumsticks carefully into the hot
     oil one at a time, on the side of the saucepan furthest from you
     (to avoid splashes), and cook them for 12–15 minutes until they are
     golden brown. Try to avoid overcrowding and fry in batches
     if necessary.

7.   Lay the cooked drumsticks on kitchen paper to soak up any excess
     oil. Finish with a pinch of salt while the chicken is still piping hot.

Sweet Stuff

Lemon and Blueberry Loaf Cake

There's a nice combination of lemons and blueberries in this recipe – it's a really tasty cake that you can make with very little fuss or messing around. It's fresh and zesty and is great paired with a cup of tea mid-afternoon.

VEGETARIAN

Ingredients

175g baking spread, plus extra for greasing

175g granulated sugar

3 medium eggs

100ml natural yoghurt

zest and juice of 2 lemons, from a budget range

200g self-raising flour

80g blueberries, from a budget range

Method

1. Preheat the oven to 180°C/160°C fan/gas mark 4. Grease and line a 30 x 15cm loaf tin or pan.

2. Put the baking spread and sugar in a bowl and beat them together until they are light and fluffy. Add the eggs and yoghurt and whisk everything together until smooth.

3. Add the lemon zest and mix it through, then add 190g of the flour and mix until you have a smooth cake batter.

4. Put the remaining flour into a small bowl and add 65g of the blueberries. Coat them in the flour, then tip everything into the cake batter and fold in.

5. Pour the batter into the loaf tin, scatter the remaining blueberries over the top and bake it in the oven for 40–45 minutes, or until a skewer inserted into the centre comes out clean.

6. Poke several small holes in the cake and squeeze the lemon juice over the top so it penetrates the cake. You can decorate with some lemon zest if you like.

7. Leave it to cool, slice and serve.

🧺 IN THE BASKET

BAKING SPREAD: based on 500g tub

SUGAR: based on 1kg bag

EGGS: based on box of 6

YOGHURT: based on 500g tub

FLOUR: based on 1.5kg bag

Chocolate Concrete Cake with Chocolate Custard

I love a bit of concrete cake! It's a cross between a cake and a biscuit, and paired with chocolate custard it's a properly tasty dessert. For £4.72 (at the time of writing) you can buy all the ingredients and there will be enough left over to make it another three or four times. You can even use the leftover ingredients to make other desserts!

VEGETARIAN

Ingredients

200g plain flour

140g granulated sugar

30g cocoa powder

100g baking block (or butter, if you have it), plus extra for greasing

500g ready-made custard

100g milk chocolate, broken into pieces

50g dark chocolate, broken into pieces

Method

1. Preheat the oven to 180°C/160°C fan/gas mark 4. Grease and line a 20 x 20cm baking tray with baking paper and set aside.

2. Combine the flour, 130g of the sugar and the cocoa powder in a bowl.

3. Melt the baking block in a saucepan on a low heat or in the microwave. Tip it into the dry ingredients and roughly mix them together. Use your hands to work the mixture until it is similar to the texture of soil.

4. Tip the mixture into the baking tray and press it down with the back of a spoon until it's completely compact. Splash 2 tablespoons of water on the top (to help it go crunchy) followed by the remaining 10g of sugar.

5. Bake the cake in the oven for 20–22 minutes until it's cooked, then take it out and allow it to cool completely.

6. To make the chocolate custard, put a pan on a low heat and pour in the custard. As it warms up add the milk and dark chocolate pieces. Keep stirring until all the chocolate has melted and there are no lumps.

7. Cut the cake into squares and serve with a few spoonfuls of custard.

IN THE BASKET

FLOUR: based on 1.5kg bag

SUGAR: based on 1kg bag

COCOA POWDER: based on 250g tub

BAKING BLOCK: based on 500g tub

Biscuit Spread Traybake Cake

Here's a very basic cake recipe – and all you need to make it is four ingredients: biscuit spread (similar to Biscoff spread), eggs, baking powder and white chocolate. It really is as simple as that, but that doesn't mean it's lacking in flavour! It's an incredibly soft, spongy and indulgent cake. Give it a go – I promise you it will be a winner.

VEGETARIAN

Ingredients

oil or baking spread, for greasing
370g smooth biscuit spread
3 medium eggs
2 tsp baking powder
100g white chocolate

Method

1. Preheat the oven to 180°C/160°C fan/gas mark 4. Grease and line a 25 x 15cm baking tray with some baking paper.

2. Mix 350g of the biscuit spread, the eggs and the baking powder in a bowl until smooth. Pour the mixture into the baking tray and bake in the oven for 18–20 minutes. When it's cooked, leave it to cool completely.

3. To decorate, melt the white chocolate in a microwave in 30-second bursts until smooth and drizzle it over the top of the cake. Repeat with the remaining 20g of biscuit spread and drizzle that over too.

4. Remove the cake from the baking tray, cut into squares and serve.

IN THE BASKET

BISCUIT SPREAD: based on 400g tub

EGGS: based on box of 6

BAKING POWDER: based on full tub

Strawberry Waffles

Breakfast or dessert? It could be either. What's important is that these waffles are good enough to eat at any time of day! For this recipe I put the strawberries inside the waffles to give a nice pop of flavour when you bite into it. Top it with more chopped strawberries for a properly fruity waffle. Strawberries are quite expensive, so I use a budget range, which is cheaper. You can add a few optional extras if you have them, such as vanilla extract and a slab of butter on top at the end.

VEGETARIAN

Ingredients

260g plain flour

70g granulated sugar

1 tbsp baking powder

½ tsp salt

480ml whole milk

2 medium eggs

1 tsp vanilla extract (optional)

60g strawberries (from a budget range) finely chopped, plus extra for topping,

cooking spray

Method

1. Preheat the waffle maker until it's piping hot.
2. Put the flour, sugar, baking powder and salt in a mixing bowl and mix until nicely combined.
3. Pour the milk into a jug, crack in the eggs and add the vanilla extract, if using. Whisk until everything is combined.
4. Gradually add the liquid ingredients to the dry mixture, whisking continuously. You want the batter to be as smooth as possible.
5. Add the strawberries and leave the mixture to sit for 5 minutes.
6. When the waffle maker is hot, spray on some cooking spray to prevent the waffles sticking. Pour in the batter to the recommended level, close the lid and cook for 5–6 minutes (cooking times vary between brands so keep your eye on them).
7. When the waffles are beautifully golden, take them out and repeat until you have used all the batter. I use a square waffle maker and usually make 6 waffles with this quantity of mixture.
8. Top the waffles with a lots of chopped strawberries and serve. You could also dust with icing sugar before serving if you have any in the cupboard.

🗑 IN THE BASKET

FLOUR: based on 1.5kg bag

SUGAR: based on 1kg bag

BAKING POWDER: based on full tub

MILK: based on 1 pint bottle

EGGS: based on box of 6

Banana Bread

This very simple five-ingredient banana bread recipe tastes like the real deal. I use raisins but you could substitute chocolate chips instead, or even pimp it up with some dried fruits. All the ingredients came to £4.15 (at the time of writing) with enough left over to make it three more times (you'd just need to buy some more bananas). You can decorate it any way you like – I tend to keep it simple and slice a banana to place on top – but if you're feeling fancy you can caramelise pieces of banana in the leftover sugar in the frying pan and place them on top.

VEGETARIAN

Ingredients

oil or baking spread, for greasing
4 ripe bananas
2 medium eggs
155g granulated sugar
270g self-raising flour
100g raisins

Method

1. Preheat the oven to 180°C/160°C fan/gas mark 4. Grease and line a 30 x 15cm loaf tin with baking paper and set aside.
2. Put 3 bananas in a mixing bowl and mash them until they're mostly smooth. Add the eggs and sugar and mix them with the bananas until they're combined.
3. Add the flour and raisins and mix again until everything is nicely combined.
4. Pour the mixture into the loaf tin and bake for 45–50 minutes.
5. Leave the loaf to cool, then decorate the top with sliced banana. Slice and serve.

IN THE BASKET

EGGS: based on box of 6
SUGAR: based on 1kg bag
FLOUR: based on 1.5kg bag
RAISINS: based on 500g bag

Chocolate Spread Brownies

I know there are a few people who don't like this word, but the only word that describes these brownies is moist. You only need 5 ingredients and about 30 minutes of your day (including prep) to make these delicious bad boys. If you have kids, get them involved too. I've found that involving your kids when cooking means that they are more likely to eat the finished product (not that they need an excuse to eat these!). The chocolate spread I use for this recipe is Aldi's version of Nutella (called Nutoka), a hazelnut-flavoured chocolate spread which is really nice – and far easier on the bank balance.

VEGETARIAN

Ingredients

oil or baking spread, for greasing
2 medium eggs
300g hazelnut chocolate spread
65g plain flour, sieved
45g milk chocolate chips
45g white chocolate chips

Method

1. Preheat the oven to 180°C/160°C fan/gas mark 4. Grease and line a 20 x 20cm baking tray with some baking paper and set aside.
2. Crack the eggs into a mixing bowl and whisk them until smooth. Add the hazelnut chocolate spread and mix well, then add the flour and gently mix it through until combined. Add the milk and white chocolate chips, folding them in until they are mixed through.
3. Pour the mixture into the baking tray and bake for 16–18 minutes until it's cooked through. Test to see whether it's cooked by poking in a wooden skewer or knife; if it comes out almost clean the brownie is cooked.
4. Leave the brownie to cool and then cut it into bite-sized chunks.

IN THE BASKET

EGGS: based on box of 6

CHOCOLATE SPREAD: based on 400g tub

FLOUR: based on 1.5kg bag

Jam and Sponge Pudding

This takes me back to school traybake cake days – it's a properly moist bit of sponge with a jam base. I love the simplicity of it and it truly is a treat. My kids absolutely love it too! I have to keep it where they can't reach it on the top shelf of the fridge, otherwise it would be gone within a couple of hours of coming out of the oven. If you want to take it up a level you could add some dried coconut shavings, chocolate chips, sprinkles or even dried fruits. I serve it with ready-made custard which works beautifully.

VEGETARIAN

Ingredients

175g baking spread, plus extra for greasing

175g self-raising flour

175g granulated sugar

3 medium eggs

1 tsp vanilla extract

200g strawberry jam, plus extra to serve

decorative sprinkles, to serve (optional)

300ml ready-made custard

Method

1. Preheat the oven to 200°C/180°C fan/gas mark 6. Grease and line a 20 x 30cm baking tray.

2. Put the baking spread, flour, sugar, eggs and vanilla extract in a bowl and beat them together until smooth.

3. Spread the jam evenly over the bottom of the baking tray. Carefully pour in the cake batter and spread it gently over the jam.

4. Bake in the oven for 20–25 minutes.

5. Take out the cake and let it cool. Spread more jam on top and add decorative sprinkles, if using.

6. Warm the custard and serve it with the cake.

🗑 IN THE BASKET

BAKING SPREAD: based on 500g tub

FLOUR: based on 1.5kg bag

SUGAR: based on 1kg bag

EGGS: based on box of 6

VANILLA EXTRACT: based on 38ml bottle

JAM: based on 500g jar

Cinnamon Blondies

When you're working to a budget you have to be creative and experiment so you spend as little as possible but can still enjoy food with great flavours. These cinnamon blondies are a good example: I've stripped the recipe back to basics but they still taste authentic! If you can spend a little extra you could top them with nuts or add dried fruit – or decorate with sprinkles. Whatever you want to do is fine; you make the rules in your kitchen!

VEGETARIAN

Ingredients

125g baking spread, plus extra for greasing
200g white chocolate, broken into chunks
150g dark brown sugar
2 medium eggs
95g plain flour, sifted
70g self-raising flour, sifted
1 tsp ground cinnamon

Method

1. Preheat the oven to 170°C/150°C fan/gas mark 3. Grease and line a 20 x 20cm baking tray.
2. Put a pan on a low heat and add the spread, stirring until it has melted, then remove the pan from the heat. Add 100g of the chocolate and stir until it has melted and is smooth.
3. Add the sugar and mix until combined, then crack in the eggs and whisk until everything is smooth.
4. Add both types of flour along with the cinnamon and stir until smooth, then add the rest of the chocolate.
5. Pour the mixture into the baking tray and bake for 45 minutes, or until a skewer inserted into the centre comes out clean.
6. Leave to cool in the baking tray and cut into squares for serving.

🗑 IN THE BASKET

BAKING SPREAD: based on 500g tub

SUGAR: based on 500g bag

EGGS: based on box of 6

FLOUR: based on 1.5kg bag

CINNAMON: based on full jar

Churros with Chocolate Sauce

These churros are big, fat, chunky sticks of sugary indulgence. The beauty of this recipe is that you can make them as big or small as you like; you can buy various piping nozzles to make different styles and shapes so you can make them the way you like them. There will be quite a few surplus ingredients despite the budget so you can just keep making more and more! You will need a deep-fat fryer, or a saucepan and a cooking thermometer, as well as oil for deep frying, but the oil can be cooled and stored so you can use it five or six times.

MAKES 10

VEGETARIAN

Ingredients

280g plain flour

¼ tsp salt

2 tsp baking powder

1 litre vegetable oil, for deep frying,
    plus 2 tbsp extra

35g granulated sugar

1 tsp ground cinnamon

150ml double cream

150g cooking chocolate

Method

1. Put the flour, salt and baking powder in a large bowl and mix them until nicely combined. Gradually add 300ml boiling water, mixing as you add it so the dough starts to come together.

2. Add the oil to give it a wet and sticky consistency. Transfer the dough to a piping bag with a patterned nozzle.

3. Heat the oil in a deep-fat fryer to 180°C and very carefully pipe the dough into the hot oil, cutting it into lengths with a pair of scissors (it's up to you how long or short you make them). Deep fry the churros for 4–5 minutes until they are golden brown. If you don't have a deep-fat fryer, heat 1 litre oil in a large saucepan to 180°C. Pipe the churros carefully into the hot oil, and cook them for about 4–5 minutes until they are golden brown. Try not to overcrowd the pan; cook the churros in batches.

4. While they are cooking; mix together the sugar and cinnamon and sprinkle it on a baking tray or large plate.

5. As soon as you remove the churros from the pan roll them in the sugar and cinnamon mixture so they are generously coated.

6. Make a simple chocolate sauce by putting a pan on a low heat and adding the cream and chocolate. Keep stirring until the chocolate has completely melted and is beautifully silky. You are now ready to serve.

🗑 IN THE BASKET

FLOUR: based on 500g bag

BAKING POWDER:
based on 30g sachet

SUGAR: based on 500g bag

CINNAMON: based on full jar

DOUBLE CREAM: based on
150ml tub

Peanut Butter and Chocolate Oat Bars

These are sweet and salty bars of chocolatey goodness. The only problem with this recipe is that you'll probably wish you'd made more of them. These bad boys never last long in my house; as soon as I've taken them out of the tray and started cutting them up the kids are pulling on my arms telling me to hurry up so they can get stuck in!

VEGETARIAN

Ingredients

380g peanut butter
190g honey
400g porridge oats
200g milk chocolate, broken into chunks
40g salted peanuts, roughly chopped

Method

1. Put the peanut butter and honey in a microwave-safe bowl and microwave on full power in 30-second bursts until you have a silky, glossy and smooth mixture.

2. Take out the bowl and gradually stir in the oats until they are well combined with the honey and peanut butter mixture.

3. Line a baking tray with cling film. I use a 25 x 18cm rectangular tray about 4cm deep. You could also use a square tray or anything that's a similar size.

4. Tip the peanut butter and oat mixture into the tray and press it down gently with the back of a spoon into the bottom of the tray. Put the tray in the fridge for 1 hour to set.

5. Microwave the chocolate in a bowl on full power in 30-second bursts until it has melted. Tip it on top of the oats, smoothing it with the back of a spoon. Sprinkle the peanuts on top.

6. Put the tray back in the fridge for a further hour until the chocolate is firm.

7. Cut into squares or rectangular bars and serve.

IN THE BASKET

HONEY: based on 340g jar
OATS: based on 1kg bag
PEANUTS: based on 200g bag

Notes

Index

Thank you

I want to say a huge thank you to each and every one of you for showing me so much support over the past few years. What started off as a few TikTok cooking videos has now grown into something incredibly special ... I keep having to rub my eyes to check I'm not actually dreaming. I've been absolutely blessed to be given the opportunity to write this book and I owe it all to my followers for supporting me and showing so much love on my videos and posts. I really hope you enjoy getting stuck into this book and it gives you the confidence to get in the kitchen and cook up some proper showstopper budget food. Of course, I hope it saves you a couple of quid on your shopping bill as well!

....

I'd like to say a special thank you to HarperCollins and Emily Sweet Associates for bringing this book to life. Without them, none of this would have ever been possible. They have been incredible. Also a massive thank you to Tom Regester, Esther Clark and Max Robinson for all the hard work they have done behind the scenes with the food photography and styling. Just look at the absolute state of it; it's simply a work of art.

....

Finally, a massive thank you to my kids and partner for being the guinea pigs for all the food tasting. They have been my personal food critics throughout all of the recipe testing and their input has been so important to help me get as much flavour as possible out of our fiver budget!

....

I'd like to dedicate this book to my kids:

Maybe, just maybe, when they grow up, they might actually think their dad was pretty cool once upon a time.